Maine Cottages

Fred L. Savage
and the Architecture of Mount Desert

John M. Bryan
Photographs by Richard Cheek

Princeton Architectural Press, New York

Dedicated to Charles Butt

who has restored Fred L. Savage's shingle-style masterpiece Rosserne, and whose generous support made possible this study of the architect's life and work.

Published by
Princeton Architectural Press
37 East Seventh Street
New York, New York 10003

For a free catalog of books, call 1.800.722.6657.
Visit our Web site at www.papress.com.

Frontispiece and page 15: Sunset over Somes Sound, Mount Desert Island
Pages 4–5: Harborside, Northeast Harbor

Project coordination: Jan Cigliano
Editing and layout: Nicola Bednarek
Design: Jan Haux

Special thanks to: Nettie Aljian, Janet Behning, Megan Carey, Penny (Yuen Pik) Chu, Russell Fernandez, Clare Jacobson, John King, Mark Lamster, Nancy Eklund Later, Linda Lee, Katharine Myers, Lauren Nelson, Jane Sheinman, Scott Tennent, Jennifer Thompson, Joseph Weston, and Deb Wood of Princeton Architectural Press —Kevin C. Lippert, publisher

Library of Congress Cataloging-in-Publication Data:
Bryan, John Morrill.
  Maine cottages : Fred L. Savage and the architecture of Mount Desert / John M. Bryan ; photographs by Richard Cheek.
      p. cm.
  Includes bibliographical references and index.
  ISBN 1-56898-317-4 (alk. paper)
  1. Savage, Fred L., 1861–1924—Criticism and interpretation. 2. Cottages—Maine—Mount Desert Island.
3. Architecture—Maine—Mount Desert Island—19th century. 4. Architecture—Maine—Mount Desert Island—20th century. I. Title: Fred L. Savage and the architecture of Mount Desert. II. Savage, Fred L., 1861–1924. III. Title.
  NA737.S325B79 2005
  728'.37'092—dc22
                                                                            2004025905

Contents

Foreword

Robert R. Pyle

Our sense of place and community is made up of memories—personal memories of first-hand experience; oral memories that recount our ancestors' experiences; and formal, codified civic memories set down in laws, ceremonies, and rituals. Together they are vital building blocks of citizenship. In a vivid and meaningful way this book preserves memories relevant to understanding the roots of communities on Mount Desert Island, Maine.

The surnames of many of Mount Desert's earliest settlers are still found in today's telephone directories. In these families many oral traditions are passed down from generation to generation, building outward from a historical core like the rings of a tree. "Dad used to farm this field," Fred L. Savage's great-nephew Don Phillips told me once, gesturing toward an alder growth. "His father grew vegetables for the hotel, and my great-grandfather grew grains. This road used to go right on up over the hill, and they used it to move the cemetery up there from where the hotel is now."

Describing the field, Don ignores the alders and the towering evergreens beyond them, for in his mind's eye he sees yellow, waving wheat and rye, bare ground, and a narrow cart track leading up the hill into the distance, on which his ancestors transported the remains of their own forebears to a new resting place. Oral traditions, living memory, set the stage for him, and he accepts the reality of things he has never seen.

Too often we assume that small-town libraries only exist to provide recreational reading. This definition is much too narrow, however, as many libraries contain local archives, images, and unpublished materials that can put us in touch with history. These collections often corroborate, focus, and vivify oral traditions; they can serve as a solid, factual foundation for civic memory.

For many years I have had the privilege of being librarian for the Northeast Harbor Library. As such, I have been a link in the chain of custody for many of the architectural records of Fred L. Savage, whose widow preserved the contents of his office in 1924. In 1985 Lewis E. Gerrish, Jr., and his family saved drawings by Savage that they found in a house in Bar Harbor and donated those related to the town to the Jesup Memorial Library in Bar Harbor and the remainder of the collection to the Northeast Harbor Library. (The Jesup library's drawings were subsequently transferred to the Mount Desert Historical Society.) Anyone interested in Savage or Mount Desert's history is indebted to Earle G. Shettleworth, Jr., Maine's State Historic Preservation officer, and the architectural historians working for him—Roger Reed and T. Mark Cole—for they initiated and supported Gerrish's donation; this not only saved the drawings but also allowed us to link them to other historical collections through a database cataloguing system. Now John Bryan has made our collection even more meaningful by anchoring it to the land and to local and national architectural and recreational trends.

While the traditional oral memory of Savage lives on, the details of his life and work have become increasingly blurred since his death in 1924. Using all sorts of evidence—the footnotes are well worth reading—this book places Savage, a native of the Asticou settlement in Northeast Harbor, in a broad context. Everyone who loves Mount Desert Island will find this an important story, for Savage, more than anyone else, shaped the architectural environment that contributes to our sense of community.

Acknowledgments

With the rarest exceptions, the death of each human individual is followed in a short time by complete oblivion.... Even family recollection or tradition quickly becomes dim, and soon fades utterly away ... men accounted famous at their deaths slip from living memories and become mere shadows or word-pictures ... which too often distort or misrepresent the originals. [1]

The memory of Fred L. Savage (1861–1924) almost slipped into oblivion. In 1954 Lewis E. Gerrish, Jr.'s, family saved architectural drawings they found in a home they bought in Bar Harbor, Maine. The house had belonged to Savage, and by saving his drawings the Gerrishes provided a wonderful lens through which we can examine Savage's career, the growth of tourism on Mount Desert Island, and the architectural development of Northeast Harbor and Bar Harbor. Today the drawings are in the collections of the Northeast Harbor Library and the Mount Desert Island Historical Society. The Bar Harbor Historical Society also preserves evocative objects and images related to Savage's work.

I am grateful to Sam McGee, a descendant of the architect, who initiated this project by showing me the drawings and some of the houses designed by Savage. For two summers, Robert R. Pyle, head of the Northeast Harbor Library, provided unfettered access to the Gerrish Collection and other unpublished material. The Northeast Harbor librarians, Judith Blank, Anna C. Carr, Windy Kearney, Tina Hawes, and Anne Haynes, were always helpful and made me feel at home. Jaylene B. Roths, the executive director of the Mount Desert Historical Society; her assistant, Heather Sisk; and Mary H. Jones, president of the society, made it possible for me to work in the society's collections; Deborah Dyer, director of the Bar Harbor Historical Society, facilitated work in Bar Harbor and made available many important historic images. George Hartman, architect, and Jan Cigliano, former editor for Princeton Architectural Press, introduced the project to Charles Butt, and his generous support made it possible to do the work and publish the book. Jan also arranged for Richard Cheek of Boston to do the new architectural and landscape photography. His beautiful photographs show the splendor of the setting that provided the cornerstone of Savage's career and illustrate why artists and rusticators came to Mount Desert.

Readers interested in the history of Mount Desert benefit from the earlier, ground-breaking research of Earle G. Shettleworth, Jr.; T. Mark Cole; and Roger G. Reed. As director of the Maine Historic Preservation Commission, Shettleworth has written, published, and sponsored research that establishes the context of Savage's career. Working for the commission during the summers of 1984 and 1985, Cole conducted architectural surveys of early summer cottages on Mount Desert. His work was followed by Reed, who combed through newspapers and compiled a list of architects, builders, and major cottages built in Bar Harbor prior to World War II. I am grateful for their work and generosity and hope they are pleased with my addition to their foundation.

Savage is remembered primarily for the summer cottages he designed during the period from around 1885 to 1924. We are grateful to the current owners whose interest in the project and permission to visit and photograph their houses has been crucial to the project. Several owners have asked to remain anonymous, but I want to publicly thank David Ames; Robert and Catherine Barrett; Charlotte Beers Beadleston; Mr. and Mrs. Curtis L. Blake; Edward Blair; James A. Blanchard; Norman Beecher; Marion Burns; James Crofoot; Mr. and Mrs. Shelby Davis; Michael Dennis; Elizabeth P. Donnan; Samuel Eliot; Theodore Eliot; Richard Estes; Jared Morris Grace; Dr. William R. Grace; C. Boyden Gray; Clark and Windy Grew; Mr. and Mrs. Fred Halbach-Merz; Robert Harry; Dr. John P. Hoche; Meriwether Hudson; Nancy Keefe; Lila Kirkland; Anne Kuckro; John Robert Lindsay; Clement McGillicuddy; Alice O. Miller; Michael Miles; Thomas Morris; Meriwether Morris; William B. Morris; Janneke Seton Neilson; Mr. and Mrs. Stephen O'Leary; Elizabeth Rendeiro; Mr. and Mrs. Bayard H. Roberts; Jared I. Roberts; Sydney Rockefeller; Louise B. Roomet; John H. Schafer; William C. Scott; Mr. and Mrs. John Sweet; Caroline, David, and Michael Stevens; Robert A. Taylor; Barbara J. Trimble; the Van Alen family; Elizabeth White; and Henry F. White.

In Northeast Harbor Robert R. Pyle, Sam McGee, Rick Savage, and Erika Wibby have been especially helpful. Among other things, they each read the draft and made constructive suggestions. Rick Savage and Sam McGee generously made family documents, photographs, and research available. Tina Hawes helped set up the files in the Northeast Harbor Library. In Bar Harbor the work has been enriched by the local knowledge and enthusiasm of Beth Whitney; in addition to reviewing drafts, she took time to take us to a number of sites. Rick Savageau, general manger of the Asticou Inn, has been very helpful. Conversations about Savage's life with Rick Savage, Edd and Brian Hamor, Raymond Strout, Roc Caivano, Rose P. Ruze, Mary H. Jones, and Theodore and Galen Turner have been productive. Others who have made substantial contributions include Mary Beth Dorsey of the Ellsworth, Maine, library; Charles A. Birnbaum, coordinator of the Historic Landscape Initiative of the National Park Service; Janet Anderson of the Islesboro Town Office; Tom Marcil and Kate Boyd, reference librarians at the University of South Carolina; Lindsay Smith, who has done much of the Internet research; Michele Clark at the Frederick Law Olmsted archives; and my friend and colleague Hunter Clarkson, who did the archival photography.

I am especially grateful to Martha, my wife, who worked in the Mount Desert Historical Society Archives and processed the data that allowed me to compile the preliminary list of Savage's buildings (see Appendix). Our daughter Molly initiated the whole project by suggesting that I contact her friend Sam McGee, and she often provided a home away from home during research trips to Mount Desert. I hope this book contributes in a general way to the understanding, appreciation, and preservation of the island and its environs. More specifically, I hope it pleases everyone who contributed, especially the cottage owners, Savage's descendants, and Molly and all of her Maine family.

Introduction

Fred Lincoln Savage (1861–1924) did more than anyone else to shape the architectural character of Mount Desert.[1] As a young man, he worked as a carpenter in Northeast Harbor, his hometown, before he trained as a draftsman (circa 1885–1887) in the Boston office of Peabody and Stearns.[2] He returned home in 1887, just as resort development in Northeast Harbor was gathering momentum. Surviving drawings and construction documents indicate that between 1885 and his death in 1924, he designed some three hundred buildings, most of them on Mount Desert Island. He also supervised or designed alterations for projects by other architects, including W. R. Emerson, Rotch & Tilden, and Andrews, Jacques & Rantoul of Boston; Grosvenor Atterbury of New York; Burnam & Root of Chicago; and Furness, Evans & Company of Philadelphia.[3]

Like many of his architect peers, Savage worked in several styles. His shingle-style buildings are the most memorable, however, reflecting the ideals and ideas that prompted recreational development along the coast of Maine during the late nineteenth and early twentieth centuries. For Savage's professional life coincided with the early, formative stages of tourism on Mount Desert.

When Savage was young, his family and neighbors made their living from the land and sea just as their ancestors had done for several generations. Women and children maintained the households and gardens and tended livestock. The men's work varied with the seasons. During the winter they cut timber and skidded it out on the snow; in the spring they plowed and planted, and during the summer and fall they often left home as fishermen or sailors carrying freight along the coast. Working together, families extracted a living from a challenging environment.

Writers, poets, and painters started celebrating the American landscape in the early nineteenth century, and artists began traveling to Mount Desert in the 1840s. They quickly made its rugged beauty famous. Consequently, tourists began to come shortly after the Civil War to experience for themselves the landscapes and seascapes they had admired in galleries and museums. Accommodating tourists soon became a new seasonal source of income, and this proved to be the cornerstone of Savage's architectural career. For thirty-nine years he designed cottages and hotels in a variety of styles that reflected various aspects and phases of the new industry. His career ended just as the initial boom began to fade before World War I. He saw the early privately sponsored efforts to preserve the scenic quality of the land; he witnessed the formation of Acadia National Park, and as a businessman in Bar Harbor, he participated in attempts to stave off the end of the cottage era.

Fred L. Savage at his desk, c. 1898.
Courtesy of Rick Savage.

Painting, sculpture, and most of the decorative crafts are typically created by people working alone; buildings, on the other hand, are usually the fruition of collaboration. Examining Savage's buildings, we often glimpse the sharing of ideas, skills, resources, and constraints that shaped his work, and these insights make Mount Desert more meaningful.

Chapter I

Foundations

Savage's Ancestors and Mount Desert

previous page: Magnum Donum, Bishop William C. Doane Cottage, unknown architect, Northeast Harbor, c. 1881

above: The Old House, the Climena and John Savage house, Northeast Harbor, 1820

Savage's family roots on Mount Desert reached back to the eighteenth century. His paternal great-grandfather, John Savage (circa 1756–1815), had immigrated to the colonies from Glasgow, Scotland, in 1770 at the age of fourteen and worked as a fisherman sailing out of Marblehead, Massachusetts, prior to the Revolution. In 1775 he enlisted as a private and fought against the British in the Battle of Bunker Hill (where he lost his right thumb). He also participated in the Battle of White Plains, wintered at Valley Forge, and crossed the Delaware with General Washington. He must have been viewed as an able and energetic man, since he was commissioned as commander of the schooner *Resolution* as the Revolution ended.

After the war, John Savage returned to Marblehead and in December 1786 married Sarah Dolibar, a descendant of the earliest European settlers of Marblehead.[1] In 1789 John and Sarah Savage tried to better their lot by moving to Mount Desert, then a sparsely settled, eastern frontier. They stayed several years, but their first attempt to relocate failed, and they returned to Marblehead in 1792. Five years later their second attempt was more successful, and in 1797 or 1798 they established a homestead near Little Harbor Brook adjacent the eastern entry to Northeast Harbor. The site offered fresh water, a sloping, shingled beach where small boats could be hauled and launched, and a view of Bear Island to the south. Most importantly, it linked family interests to Northeast Harbor for generations to come.

When John and Sarah Savage established their homestead—a simple cabin and a clearing for vegetables and livestock—there were only a handful of neighbors nearby. Earlier settlers were living on the shores of Blue Hill Bay, Frenchman's Bay, and Somes Sound. The earliest known settlers of Mount Desert, Abraham Somes and James Richardson and their families, had occupied the head of Somes Sound since 1761, and Somesville remained the most village-like settlement well into the nineteenth century. In 1836 it consisted of "one small store, one blacksmith shop, one shoemaker's shop, one tanyard, two shipyards, one balk mill, one saw mill, one lath mill, one shingle mill, one grist mill and one schoolhouse" and nine families.[2] Early settlers typically chose sheltered coves for their settlements, preferably places with access to fresh water and hillsides and outlying islands to break the wind. Like Somesville to the northwest, the Savage homestead offered some of these advantages; on the east side of Mount Desert Island the same could be said of a cluster of homes built adjacent Hulls Cove by John Hamor, Simon Hadley, Levi Higgins, Timothy

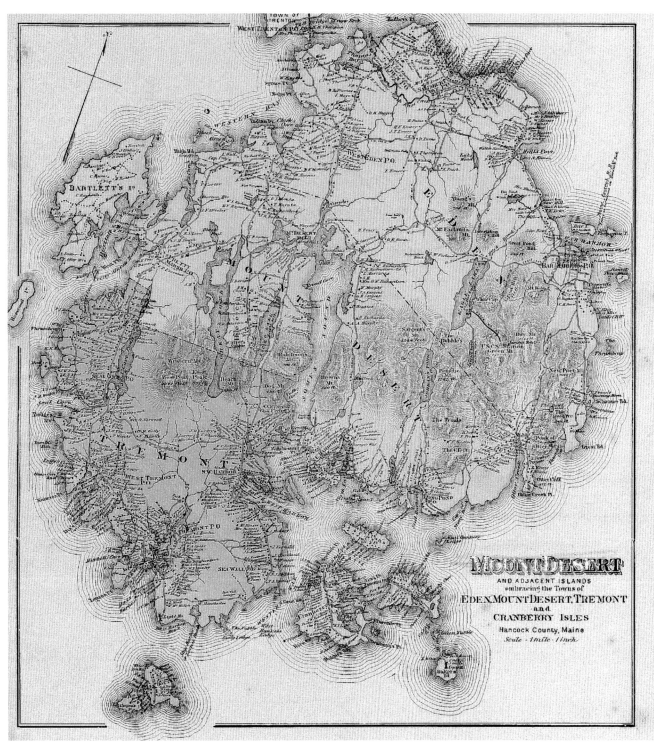

Map of Mount Desert, 1885. Courtesy of
Raymond Strout.

Smallidge, and Elisha Cousins.[3] The recreational use of the shoreline—the central pillar of Fred L. Savage's career—lay a century in the future.

Of John and Sarah Savage's seven children only one son, John Savage (1801–1868, referred to hereafter as John Savage II) remained in Northeast Harbor. In 1820 he bought a parcel of land near the head of Northeast Harbor at the present site of the Asticou Inn. Here he quickly built a house (1820) and married a seventeen-year-old neighbor, Climena Roberts. The Climena and John Savage house (now known as the Old House) has been modified by the addition of a porch and an ell, and it has been moved several times, but the core—a story-and-a-half symmetrical Cape Cod dwelling with white clapboards and modest trim—remains one of the oldest structures on Mount Desert. It is also the oldest existing building associated with the Savage family, since the first Savage cabin beside Harbor Brook seems to have been demolished or fallen into disuse in the nineteenth century. The vertically sawn sheathing and subflooring of the Old House were sawn in Somesville, whose mills were a sign of civilization signifying that frontier life in log cabins was a thing of the past.

In the Old House Climena Savage bore ten children, among them Augustus Chase Savage (1832–1911), the father of the architect, Fred L. Savage. Captain A. C. Savage, as he was called by his peers, wrote a memoir at the age of seventy in which he presents a vivid picture of his youth, of growing up in the Old House, and the daily life on Mount Desert before the Civil War. He recalls his father (John Savage II) and his neighbor Will Roberts "coasting and fishing in the summer and in winter they hauled out logs and cordwood to sell in western markets. They cut and hewed frames for their houses, rafted logs to Somesville for the boarding, sawed and shaved pine shingles for their houses and barns."[4]

A. C. Savage learned the coastal trade from his father, and until the outbreak of the Civil War, he was at sea during the temperate months, typically May through October. On various schooners he carried wood to Boston, fished off the coast of Labrador and in the Gulf of St. Lawrence, hauled freight to New York and Philadelphia, and in 1851, with the help of his father, bought his own schooner, *The Protector*. He married Emily Manchester, a neighbor whose forebears were among the first white settlers of Northeast Harbor in 1775, in 1854, and the couple moved into a new house that he had built uphill, across the road from the Old House. The A. C. Savage house, much expanded and traditionally called the Harbor Cottage, stands across the road from the present Asticou Inn. Architecturally, it was a stylistic step

forward: just as the Old House (1820) had moved beyond the functional log cabin of the 1790s, the Harbor Cottage (circa 1853–1854) with its high-pitched roof, a symmetrical plan, and porches represented a departure from the low, rectangular Cape Cod Cottage.[5]

After his marriage, A. C. Savage continued to make a voyage or two each year, ranging from Jacksonville to the Magdalen Islands. In 1863 he enlisted in the Union Navy and served in the James River campaign of 1864 to 1865. He resumed coasting after the war until 1868, when his father died. Around that time, as A. C. Savage recalls in his memoirs, "we began taking summer boarders and I may say that we were the first house to open its doors to 'Rusticators' at Northeast Harbor.[6] Among our first guests were Commodore Fyffe and family; also some noted artists, Hollingsworth, Brown and others."[7]

Fred Lincoln Savage, the third of six children born to A. C. and Emily Savage, was nine years old in 1870 when his parents began to take in rusticators. The economic value—and social, intellectual, and aesthetic values—of summer people were very much a part of his youth, and for most of his life, their comings and goings in ever increasing numbers played a significant role in the rhythm of his years.

It is not surprising that artists boarded in the Harbor Cottage during its first season as a guesthouse, nor is it surprising that A. C. Savage specifically remembered them. As a group, artists were instrumental in promoting tourism, which became the most impor-tant new source of income on Mount Desert during Fred Savage's lifetime.

23

Harbor Cottage, unknown architect,
Northeast Harbor, 1854

Artists began coming to Mount Desert in the 1840s, and through the exhibition of paintings, the reproduction of engravings and lithographs, and occasional writings, they presented Mount Desert to patrons in Boston, New York, Philadelphia, and beyond. During the 1850s, the artists were joined by people who wanted to experience the dramatic topography firsthand. Tourism dipped during the Civil War, but with that exception and another brief downturn during a recession in the early 1890s, the summer population grew steadily until World War I.

Architecturally, this new and growing industry manifested itself in several stages. During the first phase of tourism, between 1850 and 1870, local families in Somesville and the Bar Harbor area modified and expanded existing buildings to accommodate tourists—just as the Savages would do in 1870. The second phase developed momentum during the 1870s when hotels were built, often with outlying cottages.[8] The third phase saw summer people purchase land and build houses; Birch Point, the house built by Alpheus Hardy, a Boston merchant, in Bar Harbor in 1869, is often cited as the earliest. In Northeast Harbor this movement began in the summer of 1880 when Charles W. Eliot, President of Harvard, and William Croswell Doane, Episcopal Bishop of Albany, New York, purchased land and built houses of their own. Fred L. Savage would ultimately design buildings for members of both the Eliot and Doane families, and, due to a happy convergence of choice and circumstance, he was also the only architect who participated actively in every stage of the architectural evolution of tourism on Mount Desert.[9]

Birch Point, Bar Harbor, Maine—First Summer Cottage

Birch Point, unknown architect, Bar Harbor, 1869. Courtesy of the Bar Harbor Historical Society.

Architecture, like symphonic music, is essentially a social art, and to understand buildings we need to consider contributions made by many people over time. Factors that influenced nineteenth-century summer homes and hotels on Mount Desert included the initial appreciation of the setting promoted by the painters, the variety of architectural styles in vogue in America during the second half of the century, the diverse backgrounds of the summer people, and, in many cases, the architects or architectural plans they brought with them. All these factors would affect the work of Fred L. Savage.

Artists and Tourism on Mount Desert

Foreground: Widow Salisbury House, c. 1840; background: Levi Somes House, c. 1840

The early settlers had to be pragmatic about the topography of Mount Desert. They knew the dangers of the rough coast and sea-washed ledges all too well; some coves were known as safe harbors, and the forests and later the granite and even the ice were viewed primarily as marketable resources. Their buildings were essentially pragmatic too, and beyond siting, nothing about them was responsive to the landscape; instead of trying to *blend in*, the eighteenth-century Adam or Federal style and the classical revivals that followed were intentionally pristine, well-defined, self-contained assertions of culture over context. This aspect of the antebellum buildings is best seen today in Somesville, where the old styles are still dominant. Houses there typically take the form of simple boxes clad in white clapboards with symmetrically arranged windows and doors. In form, ornament, and materials, buildings erected on Mount Desert prior to about 1870 might have been built anywhere north of Boston.

The architectural changes that came in the late nineteenth century were a direct consequence of a reinterpretation of the landscape as new ideas, attitudes, and values arrived with the artists and summer people. The profound impact of this reinterpretation is visible in the contrast between the older forms in Somesville and the character of Northeast Harbor and Bar Harbor where styles favored during the late nineteenth and early twentieth centuries hold sway.

Today we take pleasure in undeveloped and rugged landscapes. The early settlers, however, saw things differently, and their point of view was shaped by more than practical difficulties.[10] The colonists typically regarded wilderness from a biblical perspective that defined the natural setting as an opponent, a state of chaos to be conquered, put in order, and made fruitful. In 1629 John Winthrop declared "earth is the lords Garden & he hath given it to the sons of men ... with a general condition, Gen. 1:28: Increase & multiply, replenish the earth & subdue it."[11]

A radically different perspective emerged during the eighteenth and nineteenth centuries. The writings of Edmund Burke (*A Philosophical Inquiry into the Origin of Our Ideas of the Sublime and the Beautiful*, 1756), Immanuel Kant (*Observations on the Feeling of the Beautiful and the Sublime*, 1764), and others elaborated on the idea of the sublime attributed to Longinus (first century A.D.) who stated that large or powerful natural phenomena such as storms, the sea, or mountains evoke awe and fear because they give us glimpses of the power of the creator. In the late eighteenth century, William Gilpin defined the alluring asymmetries and irregularities found in nature as the Picturesque, a phenomenon less dramatic but more ubiquitous than the

top: Looking south across Eagle Lake to
Pemetic Mountain, Acadia National Park

bottom: Monument Cove, Acadia
National Park

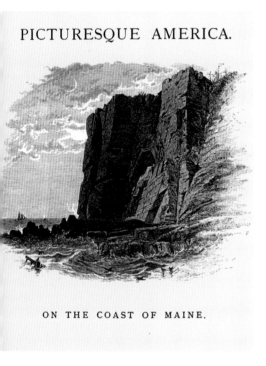

PICTURESQUE AMERICA.

ON THE COAST OF MAINE.

above: "Castle Head, Mount Desert,"
Harry Fenn, c. 1872. William Cullen
Bryant, ed., *Picturesque America* (New
York, 1872), 1.

opposite: "The 'Spouting Horn' in a
Storm," Harry Fenn, c. 1872. William
Cullen Bryant, ed., *Picturesque America*
(New York, 1872), 9.

Sublime. For Gilpin and his followers a picturesque setting possessed the attractive attributes of a tranquil landscape painting—nature at rest as it were—a setting in which everything coexists peacefully. Nineteenth-century Romantics and Transcendentalists embraced these concepts, which promised direct, individual access to universal truths. Ralph Waldo Emerson, for example, wrote that "nature is the symbol of the spirit...the world is emblematic." And making the same point, Henry David Thoreau observed that "man cannot afford to be a naturalist to look at Nature directly.... He must look through and beyond her."[12]

The writings of Thomas Cole and Frederick Church, the most famous of the nineteenth-century painters to visit Mount Desert, make it clear that they meant to illustrate these ideas. They sought the Sublime in the sculpted surfaces of Mount Desert and recorded rocks, waves, and weather in order to evoke a sense of awe and majesty. Cole noted in his journal that "the whole coast along here is iron bound— threatening crags, and dark caverns in which the sea thunders."[13] And Church described the "immense rollers [that] come toppling in, changing their forms and gathering in bulk, then dashing into sparkling foam against the base of old 'Schooner Head,' and leaping a hundred feet in the air. There is no such picture of wild, reckless, mad abandonment...as the fierce, frolicsome march of a gigantic wave."[14]

A New York critic, describing one of Church's Mount Desert paintings, wrote that

the highest triumph we remark in Mr. Church's marine [painting] is the solemnity of the sea.... His pictures have a broad and grave character—a meaning.... Whoever has been overtaken by nightfall upon the shore, and, as the twilight darkened, saw some relic of the sea's fury drifting by or lodged among the rocks, and as he looked across the heaving gloom its melancholy wail made visible, so that by sight and sound he was sympathetically enthralled—he has had that feeling of pathetic solemnity in the ocean of which Mr. Church, this year, and the last, has shown himself the Poet.[15]

In 1872 William Cullen Bryant, already famous for half a century as the preeminent poet of the American landscape, published *Picturesque America*, two large volumes, with descriptions and engravings illustrating some eighty sites from coast to coast. Bryant did not rank the sites, but he presented Mount Desert first. Engraved illustrations of the island, based on drawings by Harry Fenn, emphasized the forces of

29

"View from Via Mala at The Ovens,"
Harry Fenn, c. 1872. William Cullen
Bryant, ed., *Picturesque America* (New
York, 1872), 16.

nature, and Bryant's accompanying description articulated the new point of view just
as the wave of development was getting under way:

> The island of Mount Desert . . . unites a striking group of picturesque fea-
> tures. It is surrounded by seas, crowned with mountains, and embosomed
> with lakes. . . . It affords the only instance along our Atlantic coast where
> mountains stand in close neighborhood to the sea; here in one picture are
> beetling cliffs with the roar of restless breakers, far stretches of bay dotted
> with green islands, placid mountain-lakes mirroring the mountain-precipices
> that tower above them, rugged gorges clothed with primitive forests, and
> sheltered coves where the sea-waves ripple on the shelly beach. Upon the
> shores are masses of cyclopean rocks heaped one upon another in titanic
> disorder, and strange caverns of marvelous beauty; on the mountains are
> frightful precipices, wonderful prospects of far extending sea, and mazes of
> land and water. . . . It is a union of all those supreme fascinations of scenery,
> such as Nature, munificent as she is, rarely affords.

Bryant admonished the viewer or future visitor:

> Not one man in ten discerns half the beauty of a tree or of a pile of rocks,
> and hence those who fail to discover in a landscape the charm others
> describe in it should question their own power of appreciation rather
> than the accuracy of the delineation. The shores of Mount Desert must
> be studied with this appreciation and taste. . . . Go to the edge of the cliffs
> and look down; go below, where they lift in tall escarpments above you;
> sit in the shadows of their massive presence; study the infinite variety of
> form, texture, and color, and learn to read all the different phrases of sen-
> timent their scarred fronts have to express. When all this is done, be
> assured you will discover that "sermons in stones" was not a mere fancy
> of the poet.[16]

Many notable American painters, including Thomas Doughty (1793–1856),
Alvan Fisher (1792–1863), Fitz Hugh Lane (1804–1865), Thomas Cole (1801–1848),

"Mount Desert Rock," Thomas Doughty, 1839. Courtesy of the Mount Desert Island Historical Society.

and Frederick Church (1826–1900), worked on the island and emphasized the visual drama of mountains rising from the sea, the intimacy of folded hills and coves, the power of the waves, and—by way of contrast—the puny scale of man gauged in this setting.[17] Their works of art, exhibited in galleries or reproduced in books and magazines, made Mount Desert known to a wide circle of people, who were fascinated by its dramatic setting.

Recreation, Education, and Moral Development

Histories of Mount Desert typically cite the publicity generated by artists in the 1850s as a catalyst for tourism. We should be careful, however, not to overemphasize the artists' role, for they were part—albeit an important and highly visible part—of a larger wave of tourists who sought wild places for a variety of reasons. Vacation treks through the Adirondacks and White Mountains had become a tradition among college students in New England prior to the Civil War, for example. As the student *Harvard Magazine* put it, "These glorious long rambles...give us a new lease of health for the coming year." The outings "kindle anew the noblest aspirations of the soul," and celebrate the "glorious spirit of liberty which is ever associated with mountain regions."[18] As an undergraduate, Charles W. Eliot, who later became president of Harvard and was one of the first summer residents of Northeast Harbor, made long excursions during the summers of 1852 and 1857. He and his companions studied "geology on the ground as well as in books," walking "fifteen to twenty-five miles a day...through Nova Scotia, New Brunswick, parts of Quebec, New York State, New Jersey and some of the Pennsylvania mining regions, not to speak of parts of Maine, New Hampshire, Vermont, and the Berkshires."[19] During the summer of 1857, Harvard undergraduates George B. Chadwick and Samuel H. Eels walked from Waterville, Maine, to Quebec. Two years later, John Ritchie and Wendell Phillipps Garrison, also Harvard undergraduates, walked 286 miles, starting in western Massachusetts and hiking through the Connecticut, Housatonic, and Hudson river valleys to West Point, New York. Articles about these trips celebrated a sense of physical well-being, the freedom afforded by a change of scene, the camaraderie forged by shared experience, and pride in challenges overcome.

Thoreau made three extended camping trips into the Maine woods and wrote about them in various publications. He climbed Mount Katahdin in 1846, went moose hunting at Chesuncook and Moosehead Lake in 1853, and canoed the Allegash and East Branch of the Penobscot River to Bangor in 1857. His accounts are studded with a precise record of flora and fauna: "Beside the plants which I have mentioned, I observed on the bank here the *Salix cordata* and *rostrata* [long-beaked willow], *Ranunculus recurvatus* [hooked crowfoot], and *Rubus triflorus* [dwarf raspberry] with ripe fruit."[20] Thoreau often grounded his far-reaching philosophical observations on his examination of natural phenomena close at hand, and his interest in the world around him was shared by many people. During the nineteenth century the physical sciences—botany, ornithology, ichthyology, mineralogy—gained in importance, and

their practitioners were actively finding, naming, categorizing, and studying components of the American landscape. Trips into the wilderness were thus as often inspired by an urge to learn more about our natural surroundings as to promote one's health and moral development.

Mount Desert was—and is—exciting for those interested in flora and fauna. Its bedrock has been laid bare by successive glaciers and the action of the sea; its tide pools, resembling a necklace of aquariums, exhibit numerous life forms along the shore. The bracing, salty maritime climate influenced by the Gulf of Maine and even the complexities of getting to the remote island were other factors that contributed toward making a visit to the Mount Desert exotic—a time and place apart.

The earliest widely published recreational cruise to Mount Desert encapsulates all these disparate interests that prompted the development of tourism. On July 3, 1858, the *Helen of Swampscott* got under way from the north side of Long Wharf in Boston. Aboard were Robert Carter, Washington correspondent for the *New York Tribune*, an anonymous Washington-based naturalist specializing in ichthyology (Carter calls him the Professor and mentions his participation in the North Pacific Exploring Expedition), an artist and another companion (neither are identified by name), and two paid seamen, Captain William G. Gurney of Swampscott and "old Captain Widger."[21] Carter joined the Professor's cruise to escape the heat in Washington. As an added inducement, the Professor promised to "run into every harbor from Provincetown to Eastport, and fish and dredge till you have seen at least one specimen of every creature that swims the sea or dwells on the bottom."[22]

They were becalmed before they got out of Boston Harbor, so they began fishing, but "pulled up only a sea-weed, consisting of a long, cylindrical, hollow stem, gradually expanding into a leaf some ten inches in breadth. This plant is the *Laminaria saccharina*." The Professor then methodically identified "about twenty species of marine animals, and several marine plants besides [Latin names and all], on this one piece of sea-weed, accidentally pulled from the bottom by a fish-line."[23] The cruise continued in this fashion—a veritable marine biology course.

Ultimately, the *Helen* landed at Bass Harbor, the southernmost harbor on Mount Desert. Carter and two companions walked to South West Harbor where they spent the night with a deacon before they drove on to Bar Harbor and found lodging with the postmaster. For two days they explored Otter Creek, Great Head, and Schooner Head "which make the island so fascinating to the landscape and marine painter."

Looking north from Otter Cove toward Cadillac and Dorr Mountains, Acadia National Park

Carter noted that selective forestry and conservation "would make this island, with its mighty cliffs and somber ravines and multitudinous ocean beaches, a place of pilgrimage from the ends of the earth, to all lovers of the beautiful and sublime in nature. It is impossible to conceive of any finer field for the exercise of the highest genius of the landscape gardener."[24] Vacation over, Carter boarded a steamer in Bar Harbor, bound for Rockland and Boston.

After the Civil War improved transportation—first steamboats and then railroads—made Mount Desert increasingly accessible as a vacation destination. The first scheduled steamboat landed in Bar Harbor in 1857, and until 1884 the typical tourist reached the island as a passenger aboard a steamer from Rockland, Maine. In 1884, the Maine Central Railroad opened express service from Boston. The train ran six days a week during the summer and connected in Trenton, Maine, with steamers owned by the railroad. Passengers completed the journey with an eight-mile boat trip down Frenchman's Bay to Bar Harbor. The train-boat combination was an instant success: in 1885 the steamers carried 12,299 passengers in addition to freight; the following year they carried 17,440 passengers, and in 1887 they carried 24,872 people. (The Maine Central express service ended in 1931. After World War II tourism would be based on the use of privately owned automobiles.)

Rusticators Come
to Northeast Harbor

THE RODICK.
LARGEST HOTEL IN MAINE. FOUR HUNDRED SLEEPING ROOMS
BELONGING TO THIS HOTEL
Also a NUMBER of COTTAGES connected therewith. Complete Drainage and Water
Supply. Highest Elevation and most beautiful and extensive views. LARGEST LAWN
and GROUNDS of any hotel at Bar Harbor.
Lighted with Gas, and has all Modern Improvements.
☞ Our Halls, Parlors, Offices, and Dining Hall, afford ample accommodation for One
Thousand Persons.
☞ Prices according to size and location of rooms. Liberal terms by the Season.
D. RODICK & SONS, - - - - - - - **Bar Harbor, Maine.**

Tourism had been under way in Bar Harbor and its environs for several decades before it affected life in Northeast Harbor. On September 4, 1844, the painter Thomas Cole had boarded at the Lynam Farm near Schooner Head, and the resulting publicity has prompted a historian to mark this as "the day... the Bar Harbor summer colony was founded."[25] Summer traffic increased slowly throughout the following decade. In 1850 Frederick Church, Cole's protégé, stayed with Albert Higgins in Bar Harbor, and two years later Higgins rented rooms to "the first long-term summer visitors."[26] The first hotel, the Agamont House, owned by Tobias Roberts, opened in 1855. Captain Charles Deering brought the first steamboat to Bar Harbor in 1855, and three years later he opened his own hotel there. In 1869 the *Ellsworth American* reported that 500,000 board feet of lumber had been "brought into Bar Harbor that summer, and that the sound of hammer and saw was heard from dawn to dusk."[27] By the 1870s four scheduled steamships a week were landing in Bar Harbor, coming from Portland and Rockland where travelers could make connections to Boston and points south. Reliable, scheduled transportation allowed the public at large to come in ever increasing numbers. Consequently, in 1872 Bar Harbor had fifteen hotels, and in 1888—the "high-water mark of the hotel era"—eighteen hotels could provide accommodations for 2,500 tourists. The Rodick House alone, then the largest hotel in Maine, had a capacity of six hundred.[28]

Summer visitors began to buy land and build houses in Northeast Harbor in 1880. William C. Doane, an Episcopal Bishop from Albany, New York, had already spent several summers in Northeast Harbor, staying with his family in the Kimball House, before he acquired land and built his own cottage, Magnum Donum. Joseph Henry Curtis (1841-1928), a landscape architect from Boston, bought land from A. C. Savage and began construction in 1880 on his Thuya Lodge, and Charles W. Eliot, President of Harvard College, also purchased 120 acres from A. C. Savage the same year and built a shingle-style cottage, the Ancestral. Eliot's cottage was designed by his brother-in-law, the well-known Boston architect Robert Swain Peabody (1845-1917), a proponent of the colonial revival movement. A. C. Savage did not only sell land to these early rusticators but also helped build their cottages, directing the construction of Thuya Lodge for Curtis and the Ancestral for Eliot. His 1880-1882 account book shows that he obtained labor and materials, scheduled work, and disbursed funds for both projects.[29]

Like Bishop Doane, President Eliot had summered nearby for some time before he built. In 1871, recently widowed and with two teenage sons, Charles and Samuel, he

above: Bar Harbor Wharf, c. 1890.
Courtesy of the Bar Harbor Historical
Society.

opposite top: Bar Harbor, Steamer Frank
Jones, 1905. Courtesy of the Bar Harbor
Historical Society.

opposite bottom: The Rodick, *Mount
Desert Herald*, July 12, 1883

Magnum Donum, Bishop William C. Doane Cottage, unknown architect, Northeast Harbor, c. 1881

purchased the *Jesse*, a thirty-three-foot sloop, and sailed to Mount Desert from Boston, obtaining permission to camp on uninhabited Calf Island on the east side of Frenchman's Bay opposite Bar Harbor.[30] The following year Eliot had the forty-three-foot *Sunshine* built, and with his sons, friends, and relatives, he sailed down east time and again, spending the summers of 1872, 1874, 1875, 1876, and 1878 camping on Calf Island.[31] He remarried in 1877, and in 1880 traveled with his wife to Europe while his sons spent the summer on Somes Sound with friends, vacationing and studying "geology, ornithology, marine invertebrates, meteorology, botany, entomology, ichthyology, and photography."[32] When Eliot returned from Europe, his sons pointed out the land that he would purchase from A. C. Savage later that year.

After deciding to summer in Northeast Harbor, Eliot cultivated a friendly relationship with the Savage family. As A. C. Savage's granddaughter, Emily Philips Reynolds, recalls, the Eliots were frequent visitors at the Savage home (Harbor Cottage, now called Cranberry Lodge) and were "counted as special friends."[33] A. C. Savage, a Baptist, also joined Eliot and others in establishing the Union Church in Northeast Harbor in 1886, and subsequently, when they were both elderly, President Eliot convinced A. C. Savage to allow him to have A. C.'s memoirs typed, distributed, and preserved.[34]

Fred L. Savage was nineteen years old when work began on the Eliot house. He had attended the village school in Northeast Harbor, and like most young men his age on Mount Desert, he had already worked at a variety of jobs, having been a fisherman, a postmaster, and a carpenter. His father's account book shows that in December 1880,

From left to right: the first Asticou Inn, Fred L. Savage's Hilltop Cottage, Harbor Cottage, c.1895. Courtesy of the Northeast Harbor Library.

Fred was working on the Thuya Lodge; his labor was valued at $1.25 per day (A. C. Savage was billing $1.00 per day for the use of a horse on the job). Fred first appears on the Eliot cottage payroll on April 22, 1881; here he received $1.30 per day, the daily billing rate for each of the craftsmen on the job.

As Reynolds recalls, "as a young man Fred had unusual ability in wood-carving and cabinet making, and this attracted the attention of members of the summer colony."[35] According to family tradition, President Eliot was instrumental in shaping Savage's future career by placing Fred as an apprentice in the Boston architectural office of Robert Swain Peabody around 1884.

Fred's decision to become an architect was only one aspect of his family's response to the rising tide of tourism, however. Shortly before he went to Boston, his father and older brother Herman (1855–1913) built two of the earliest hotels in Northeast Harbor. In 1883 A. C. Savage built the first Asticou Inn (burned in 1900), and Herman Savage, who was then twenty-eight years old, built the Rockend Hotel (burned in 1942). Working with local contractors, they may have planned these hotels themselves, or perhaps they worked with John E. Clark (1843–1909), an architect then active in Bar Harbor, for the original Asticou and the Rockend were similar to hotels that had transformed Bar Harbor during the previous decade.

In developing hotels with satellite cottages, the Savage family and their predecessors in Bar Harbor were repeating an architectural formula that first appeared in the colonies in the south. Rural resorts associated with healing springs, outdoor activities, and scenic topography were established in Virginia prior to the Revolution. George

Washington, for example, found more than two hundred people in tents and cabins when he visited Berkeley Warm Springs in 1761. The nineteenth-century southern resort architectural pattern consisted of a hotel containing public rooms, communal dining, and extensive porches or piazzas, surrounded by cottages for accommodation. This recognizable constellation was well developed in the antebellum period—Virginia examples include Blue Sulfur Springs, Bath Alum Springs, Fauquier Springs, White Sulfur Springs, and Red Sulphur Springs—and it spread "from Maine to California and from Florida to Idaho."[36] Beyond architectural patterns, tourism on Mount Desert shared other attributes with the earlier resorts; difficult access added to the sense of adventure, and a remote location protected the rustic setting and encouraged visitors to come for more than a short visit.[37]

View of Red Sulphur Springs, Virginia,
1836–1837, George Esten Cooke. Photo
courtesy of: The Charleston Renaissance
Gallery, Charleston, South Carolina.

Savage's Architectural Training

Between about 1884 and 1886, Savage was in Boston working as an office boy or apprentice for Peabody and Stearns.[38] The firm had been established in 1870, and by the time Savage arrived, it was among the most active and prestigious architectural offices in New England. Peabody and Stearns employed numerous draftsmen at their firm, many of whom would later establish their own architectural offices, among them Arthur Little and Robert Day Andrews.

Today Peabody and Stearns' stylistic diversity has been overshadowed by attention given the shingle style (see p. 70) and their masterpiece, Kragside, in Manchester, Massachusetts. Peabody designed Kragside—"one of the great achievements in the Shingle Style"—for George Nixon Black, and it was built (1882–1884) just prior to Savage's arrival in the office.[39] Kragside is indubitably the firm's most famous design and was described by historian Vincent Scully, who defined the shingle style, as "an integral unity between technique and expression."[40] Kragside presented design characteristics that Savage subsequently used on a less grand scale. Located in Manchester by the Sea, the cottage was sited at the top of a steep ledge above the surf; its stone retaining walls and foundations seemed an outgrowth of the rocky shore. Above its stone foundation the shingled elevations were as varied in form and silhouette as the windswept shore and vegetation. Here Savage may have seen the memorable example of bell-like ogee tower roofs, a variety of porches and dormers, and the complex juxtaposition of gabled gambrel and hipped roofs that he later used in similar settings. Much of Savage's early work would be in the shingle style, but whatever he learned from Kragside, it is important to remember that Scully goes on to say that Peabody and Stearns "never again, to my knowledge, created a house of such quality. One may wonder whether later, as they produced their cool Georgian formulas out of books, they regretted their freer early days."[41]

In the Peabody and Stearns office, Savage was exposed to a smorgasbord of styles, for Peabody was an early proponent of the colonial revival, which promoted both the irregular, picturesque vernacular traditions of the seventeenth and early eighteenth centuries and the classically based Georgian and Federal styles. In America, the colonial revival style was grounded in an antiquarian interest that grew in popularity throughout the nineteenth century. The Centennial Exhibition in Philadelphia (1876) focused attention on the nation's past, and architects such as Peabody and Stearns, Cabot and Chandler, and William Ralph Emerson, among others, began to document important colonial buildings and to incorporate elements of these buildings into their own designs. Peabody and Stearns produced Victorian Gothic churches; Queen Anne, English Baronial, and Renaissance revival residences; Richardsonian Romanesque educational facilities; and commercial buildings in a variety of styles. Peabody accepted "work of almost any kind," and "had no compunctions about designing houses in the Queen Anne style one day and in the Renaissance style the next." He "found eclecticism best suited to his needs."[42] This stylistic breadth would be a major hallmark of Savage's career as well. Besides producing numerous shingle-style cottages, the architect would also embrace a variety of historical revival styles in his designs.

Robert Day Andrews, a draftsman at the office who later became a distinguished architect, described the office setting as Savage experienced it:

> Office hours . . . were from half past eight until half past five, with an hour out at noon . . . work as office boy involved clearing off all the tables, and putting away the drawings and account books in the large vault at night, and taking them out in the morning; running out with drawings and notes to contractors' shops, and copying letters and full sizes. The latter had to be done by laying a sheet of detail paper under the drawing and pricking through all the lines, when the original was taken up and the pinpoints traced in pencil and connected. As for the letters and bill[s], because there were no typing machines they were written by hand in ink, and copied by pressing them, in a screw press, against moistened sheets of thin paper bound up in books made for the purpose. . . . Copies of specifications were all written by hand, and had to be carefully compared with the original to prevent mistakes. There was no "economy" paper, nor any blueprints; all copying involved as much manual labor as the original.[43]

The office "rarely had more than twenty or twenty-five [employees] and the 'regulars' numbered some ten or a dozen at the outside . . . they managed to get things done with an efficiency and celerity that enabled the office to accomplish as much as many an organization of two or three times their size."[44] Peabody was the principle designer, while John Stearns, who was "dynamic and vitriolic," ran the office "in an exceedingly thorough and efficient manner," and the head draftsman, Julius A. Schweinfurth, was "the envy of all draftsmen. . . . To most of us, with all due respect for the firm, he was the office itself."[45]

opposite: Carriage Road,
Acadia National Park

During the time Savage was in Boston, Peabody and Stearns worked on such commissions as the picturesque, medieval English Unitarian Church in Weston, Massachusetts (1886–88); the colonial revival Mrs. Nathan Thayer house in Boston (1884–86); the shingle-style Breakers' playhouse in Newport (1886), and the Richardsonian Romanesque Memorial Hall for the Lawrenceville School in Lawrenceville, New Jersey (1884–85). Through the task of copying, Savage would thus have learned how to produce drawings in a variety of styles. In addition to his experience as a craftsman and builder, observing the architects and draftsmen at Peabody and Stearns taught him how to run an architectural office.

The Earliest Drawings by Savage

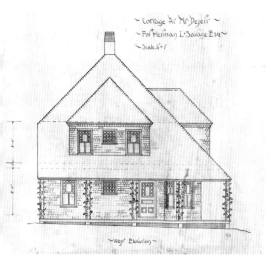

~ Cottage At Mr Dejell ~
~ For Herman L Savage Esq ~
~ Scale ¼"=1'

~ West Elevation ~

Cottage for Herman Savage, west elevation, Northeast Harbor, Fred L. Savage, 1886. Courtesy of the Northeast Harbor Library.

The earliest surviving drawings by Savage are signed "Fred L. Savage, Architect, Boston" and must have been done while he was with Peabody and Stearns. These drawings depict a cottage associated with Herman's Rockend hotel (circa 1886) and plans and elevations for the Northeast Harbor Union Church (circa 1887).[46] Considered simply as drawings, they establish a benchmark from which we can measure his growth as a draftsman and artist.

The cottage for Herman was done in watercolor on heavy paper and then refined in ink on linen. The watercolor pigments may have faded over the years, but there is no indication it ever had a variation of color intensity, or any suggestion of texture nor an illusion of space through the use of shadow or perspective. As a rendering, the cottage stands in stark contrast to an elevation of the architectural office he designed for himself in Bar Harbor (circa 1898). During the decade that elapsed between these two elevations, Savage learned how to control watercolor. He gained confidence in his ability to paint meaningful details (note the brass name plate indicated on the office door), began to use shadow to suggest three-dimensional form, and learned to lay down and preserve the integrity of small patches of color (note the windowpanes).

The simple drawing for the Rockend cottage, known as the Wedge, places young Savage in a broad and complex cultural context. The asymmetrical plan with its prominent porches reflects the influence of Andrew Jackson Downing (1815–1852) whose *Treatise on the Theory and Practice of Landscape Gardening* (1841) and *Cottage Residences* (1842) helped spark the development of the informal American suburban residence. Downing's father had established a successful nursery business at Newburgh on the Hudson River, and Downing himself was known nationally as a horticulturist before he began writing about architecture. Given his background, it is not surprising that he became the earliest American writer to stress the importance of integrating the home into its natural setting. Downing emphasized the use of porches and attached terraces as outdoor rooms; he advocated the use of natural materials and colors; and recommended the addition of projecting elements (eaves, brackets, towers, etc.) to create a broken, dappled pattern of light and shade. In general terms, the cottage for Herman, with its porches and natural building materials, was shaped—consciously or unconsciously—by Downing.[47]

The porch posts of the Rockend cottage were made of tree trunks, complete with the projecting nubs of trimmed-off limbs. These posts were carefully drawn by

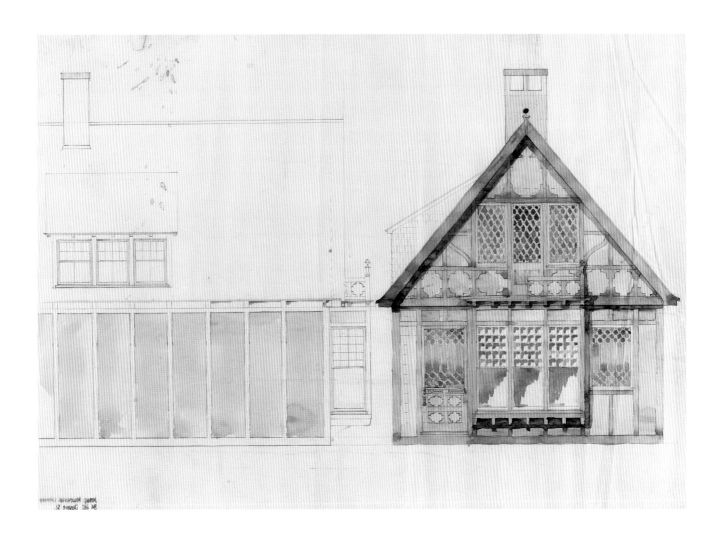

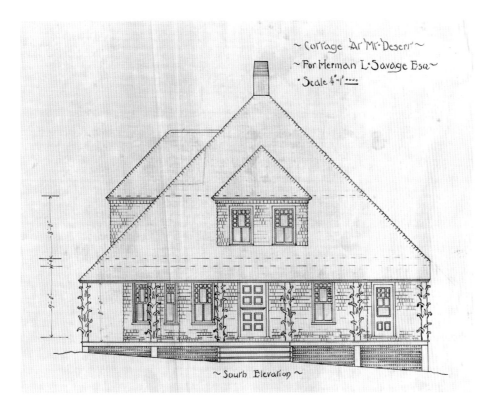

~ Cottage At Mt. Desert ~
~ For Herman L. Savage Esq ~
• Scale ¼"=1' ••••

~ South Elevation ~

top: The architectural office of Fred L. Savage, Bar Harbor, c. 1898. Courtesy of the Mount Desert Island Historical Society.

bottom: Cottage for Herman Savage, south elevation. Courtesy of the Northeast Harbor Library.

Bowditch Cottage, Putnam Camp, c. 1875.
Courtesy of the Adirondack Museum
(p11545).

Savage and are a conscious reference to the rustic style that was then especially popular in the Adirondacks; similar porch posts can be found at Camp Putnam, for example, an Adirondack camp frequented by Harvard associates of President Eliot. The rustic style was a physical manifestation of the values and beliefs that prompted urban, educated people to vacation in remote, unspoiled settings. In America, this style had its roots in the frontier cabin, and Alexander Jackson Davis (1803–1892), the New York architect who illustrated many of Downing's books, presented a rustic-style cabin as a classic temple and labeled it "American Cottage No. 1" in his own book, *Rural Residences* (1838). Since the fifteenth century, the rustic style had periodically cropped up in European architecture and literature, and there was a well-established tradition of using pseudo-primitive designs for garden grottoes and retreats—famous examples include the Grotto des Pins (1541–1543) at Fontainebleau, the Rustic Grotto or Galera (1613–1614) in the Vatican gardens, and Alexander Pope's grotto at Twickenham (circa 1725). In buildings its hallmark was always the tree-trunk columns or posts that were thought to stem from the primeval origins of architecture—the hut in the forest—as described in the famous first-century A.D. Latin text by Vitruvius, *The Ten Books of Architecture*.[48] In the eighteenth century, writer Marc-Antoine Abbé Laugiér in France and architect Sir William Chambers in England revived interest in the rustic origins of classical orders.[49]

Fred Savage may have been made aware of this style by working on Thuya Lodge, the Curtis cottage designed (1880–1881) in the rustic style by the Boston archi-tect George Moffette, Jr.[50] A. C. Savage must have been inspired by Thuya Lodge too,

"American Cottage No. 1," Alexander Jackson Davis, *Rural Residences* (New York, 1838), vol. VII, leaf 31. Courtesy of the Metropolitan Museum of Art.

for he had a small log cabin built in the woods above Asticou as "a place to go and smoke."[51] The Savages were not the only people who found Thuya Lodge attractive; Bishop Doane hired Moffette to design the first church in Northeast Harbor, St. Mary's by the Sea in 1881. Moffette's design was a hybrid rustic/stick/Scandinavian-slab style, which was replaced by the present shingle and granite St. Mary's in 1902. The exterior sheathing of the first St. Mary's consisted of bark-covered slabs, a waste by-product from local saw mills. A contemporary described it as being "in perfect keeping with its surroundings, having the charm of fitness. Built of timber, the exterior covered with spruce and hemlock slabs [the rounded outer part of logs milled for lumber], simply oiled to bring out their rich color, it looks almost as if it might have grown, so harmonious is it with its situation."[52]

Economy, informality, and simplicity motivated Bishop Doane and those who helped build the first St. Mary's, but the rustic style never became popular on Mount Desert. It was too crude to suit the tourists, and after the Rockend cottage, Fred Savage seldom used the rustic style again (the rough, slab-stone mantel in his Northeast Harbor Reading Room; the tree-trunk porch posts at Grasslands, a shingle-style cottage designed for Samuel D. Sargent; the rustic-style Random Ridge, a cottage he designed for Joseph Henry Curtis; and the organic stone steps he used at Brackenfell and Grasslands are rare exceptions). Instead, along with everyone else, he quickly turned to the shingle style, which offered a less extreme expression of similar values. Over-the-Way (1896), the second house he designed for S. D. Sargent, exemplifies the relaxed but urbane nature of his work during the next decade.

Pen and ink (a steel nib pen and indelible India ink) was another medium used by architects at the outset of Savage's career. His plans and elevations of the Union Church were drawn in pen and ink on linen (see page 59). These drawings present his ability as a draftsman while the design is attributed to Peabody and Stearns; the drawings were probably assigned to Savage because the church was to be built in his hometown.[53] The church is sited on a lot that slopes steeply up from the street. At the eastern end of the building is a complex collection of forms—a broad stone staircase, the projecting apse, the belfry, and a transept gable—that is balanced visually against the horizontal repose of the nave. This principle facade is notable for the expanse of pink and gray irregular cobblestones that form the lower wall, the vertical board-and-batten sheathing in the transept gable and belfry and the shadowed void of the porch that masks the entry. Like watercolor, pen and ink is an unforgiving medium.

above: Saint Mary's by the Sea, Northeast Harbor, George F. Moffette, 1881. Courtesy of the Northeast Harbor Library.

opposite top: A. C. Savage's "Smoking Cabin," c. 1895

opposite middle: Random Ridge, Joseph H. Curtis cottage, Fred L. Savage, c. 1890

opposite bottom: Over-the-Way, S. D. Sargent Cottage, Northeast Harbor, Fred L. Savage, 1896

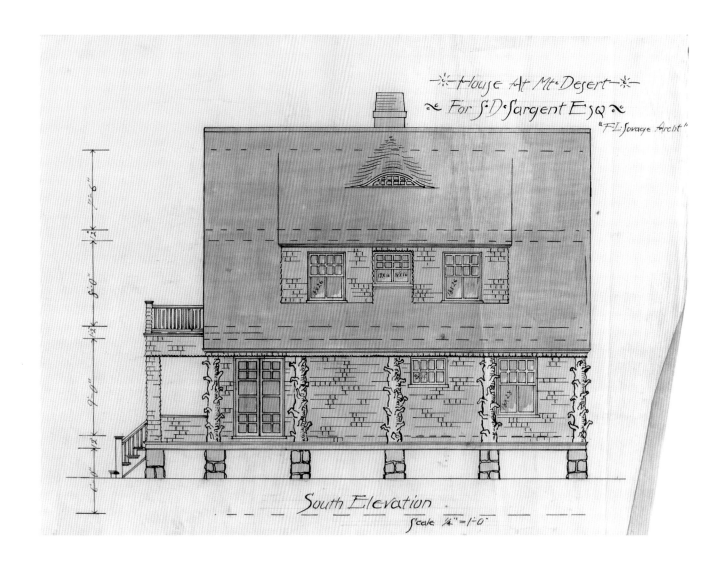

House At Mt Desert
For S·D·Sargent Esq
"F.L. Savage Archt"

South Elevation

Scale ¼" = 1'-0"

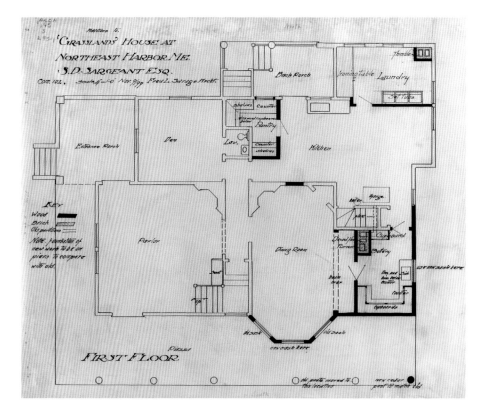

previous spread: Grasslands, S. D. Sargent cottage, Fred L. Savage, c. 1886–1888

above and right: Grasslands, south elevation and floor plan. Courtesy of the Northeast Harbor Library.

opposite: Stone steps at Grasslands

previous spread, above, and opposite:
Over-the-Way, the second S. D. Sargent
cottage, Fred L. Savage, 1896

Union Church, Northeast Harbor,
Peabody and Stearns, 1887

Savage would develop the ability to draw long, smooth lines of uniform width; to make effective use of cross-hatching to suggest mass and depth; and to construct an illusion out of the asymmetrical, seemingly random flecks, squiggles, and scratches often used by artists to convey variations of texture and surface. The Union Church drawings, however, have none of these characteristics. Instead, Savage's immaturity as a drafts-man is evident in the short, broken quality of the lines and in his failure to exploit the evocative potential of the medium. (The pen-and-ink drawings for the Pot and Kettle Club in Chapter Three provide a dramatic contrast. See p. 165.)

Approximately three thousand architectural drawings by Savage survive, and our understanding of his career is based primarily on them. In addition to sketches, which provide a record of the creative, imaginative beginnings of ideas; scaled or meas-ured plans; and sections and elevations, Savage and his peers often prepared full-size patterns of window and door casings, mantels and moldings, and other details, to guide craftsmen.

Savage's surviving drawings often illustrate his path from initial concept through construction. The artistic and intellectual exactitude, the specificity of measurement and material detail that characterize his later drawings, are missing in the early draw-ings for Herman's Rockend cottage and the Union Church. The artistic and technical shortcomings of the early drawings suggests he may have saved them as a benchmark, a memento of his time in Boston when he first called himself an architect.

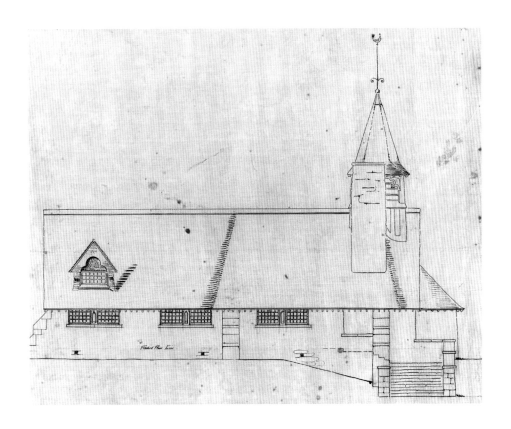

Union Church, elevations, drawn by Fred
L. Savage. Courtesy of the Northeast
Harbor Library.

Chapter II
Northeast Harbor, Islesboro, and the Shingle Style (circa 1887–1900)

Savage and Stratton, Architects

Shortly after returning from Boston, Fred Savage designed a house for himself (now called Hilltop) in the shingle style on family land across the road from the Asticou Inn.[1] It was finished by the spring of 1888, and the *Mount Desert Herald* announced, "Mr. Fred L. Savage and Miss Flora Salisbury, of Brewer, were united in marriage on Saturday, April 14th by the Rev. Dr. Torrey, of Bar Harbor. The ceremony took place in Mr. Savage's new cottage. The newly married couple gave a reception to their friends in the evening."[2] Not much is known about Flora Salisbury, who was about eighteen years old in 1888. The house Savage built for himself and his young wife served as his residence as well as his office; at the start of his career he worked there on his own, but when Savage later published this house in promotional pamphlets, in his photograph (circa 1895) a sign, "Savage and Stratton, Architects, Real Estate, Contractors," is prominently propped against the foundation.[3] This partnership with Milton W. Stratton (1871–1938) was the only partnership Savage formed during his career, and they worked together for only six years, from 1892 until 1898.

Stratton and Savage had much in common. Both were born "down east." Neither attended college. Both entered architectural offices in Boston during the 1880s, and both returned to Maine to practice. As a young man, Stratton worked with his father, a house painter in Hancock, Maine; he also worked briefly as a grocer before going to Boston where he trained in the architectural office of Little, Brown and Moore and then with Cram, Goodhue and Ferguson. According to his obituary he came to Mount Desert in 1892 to supervise a project, and immediately formed a partnership with Savage.[4]

Savage and Stratton's training was not unusual for their generation. A list of contemporary architects who were born in Maine, worked at various jobs, and then trained in architectural offices includes George W. Orff (1835–1908), William E. Barry (1846–1932), Henry Richards (1848–1949), and Antoine Dorticos (1848–1906). Dorticos trained with Francis H. Fassett, a Portland architect; the others, including Savage and Stratton, all apprenticed or worked as draftsmen in Boston.[5]

Like Savage's, Stratton's work was eclectic. His own designs outside the partnership included the classical revival–style Bar Harbor Medical and Surgical Hospital (1898); the colonial revival–style John A. Peters residence (1908) in Ellsworth, Maine; the arts and crafts–style Dr. William C. Peters residence (1911) in Bangor, Maine; the shingle-style Head Harbor Island Chapel (circa 1910); the Renaissance revival–style Lyford and Woodward Store (circa 1912) on Main Street in Bar Harbor; and the Tudor

Hilltop Cottage, Northeast Harbor, Fred
L. Savage, 1888. Courtesy of the
Northeast Harbor Library.

revival St. Edwards Convent (1916), now the home of the Bar Harbor Historical Society. Stratton left Mount Desert sometime after the partnership dissolved in 1898, establishing an office in Brookline, Massachusetts, around 1906, but he later returned to Bar Harbor, where he is listed in the 1914 telephone exchange. The following year local newspapers noted that he and his wife had taken the train to Florida where they planned to spend the winter.[6] Unlike Savage, Stratton never developed a large, sustaining clientele among the summer people.

Savage and Stratton were able to hang up their sign and begin practicing when they felt ready, since their profession was still defining itself in America, and no license was required to practice architecture in Maine. The American Institute of Architects (AIA) had been established in New York in 1857, but regional chapters, educational opportunities, and licensing requirements developed slowly across the country during the next half-century. Architects in New York established the first local chapter of the AIA in 1867, and those in other cities followed suit. Chapters were organized in Baltimore, Chicago, and Philadelphia in 1869; Cincinnati in 1870; Boston in 1871; Albany in 1874; Rhode Island in 1875; San Francisco in 1882; and Washington, Detroit, Indiana, and Central New York in 1887. Architects living in Maine were eligible to join the Boston Society of Architects; the Maine Society of Architects was not established until 1912 and did not become affiliated with the AIA until 1934. The Chicago and Illinois chapters of the AIA lobbied to obtain the earliest state licensing law in 1897. Maine organized its licensing procedures in 1945 and licensed architects for the first time in 1946.[7]

Savage did not participate in professional organizations and seems to have had little contact with his peers beyond supervising projects for architects from Boston, Philadelphia, New York, or Chicago. He based his professional life on what he had learned from Peabody and Stearns, from publications, and his own observations. He was instinctively orderly and systematic, filing drawings by rolling together everything related to a job—typically including preliminary sketches on tissue, ink on linen, and blueprints—then wrapping the roll in heavy brown paper, tying it with string, and writing the client's name on the outside.[8] He apparently began assigning sequential job numbers to projects around 1899, for in that year a house for Mrs. Giedion Scull in Northeast Harbor was labeled "commission 100." Many subsequent drawings were labeled with the project and client's name as well as the date and job number; the

Asticou Inn for A. C. Savage in 1900 was thus commission 121, the Gliman High

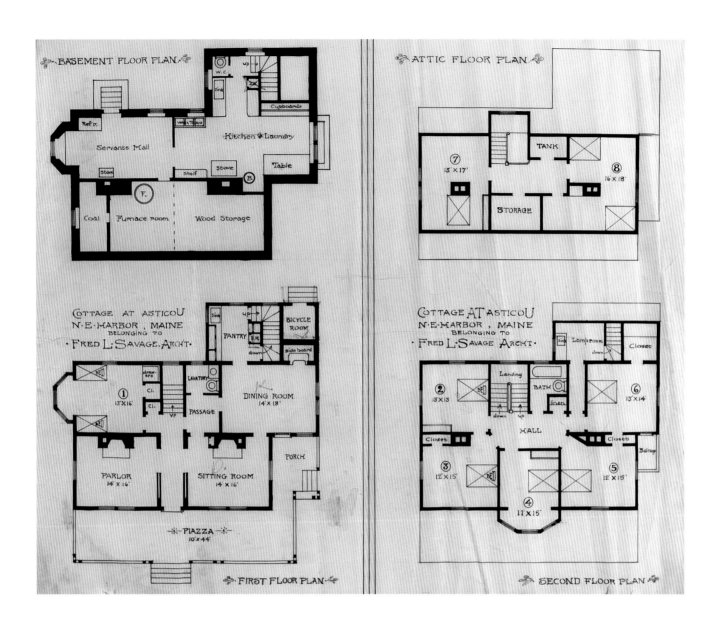

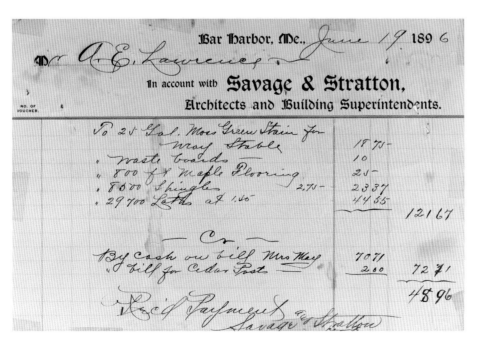

top: Hilltop Cottage, floor plans. Courtesy of the Northeast Harbor Library.

bottom: Invoice: A. E. Lawrence in account with Savage & Stratton, Architects and Building Superintendents, 1896. Courtesy of Raymond Strout.

School in 1906 for the Town of Northeast Harbor was commission 231, and the Pastime Theater in 1913 for William Dolliver was commission 281.[9]

Except for the drawings, almost none of Savage's papers survive, but local newspapers provide a narrow glimpse into the office. After practicing in Northeast Harbor for a brief time, he established himself in Bar Harbor early in his career. The *Bar Harbor Times* noted on May 24, 1893, that he was setting up an office on Main Street in second-floor rooms above B. S. Higgins Store. He worked there less than five years, for on October 18, 1899, the newspaper reported he was building an addition onto "his office on Cottage Street."[10] Here, in a building he had designed for himself, he worked for more than twenty years. On March 15, 1922, the *Bar Harbor Times* noted that the second floor of the Dunbar Block, "formerly the office of Fred Savage," that is, his first office in Bar Harbor, was being remodeled into an apartment and that Savage "is moving downstairs." At the age of sixty-one he moved back into the building where he had started his architectural practice in Bar Harbor. Perhaps he was taking in sail, for he died two years later.

Few of Savage's letters survive, but he seems intentionally to have preserved one from Agnes Platt, and it provides a glimpse into the intricacies of his relationship with clients. The letter is undated, but probably refers to the completion of Ardeen (circa 1903–1904), a Bar Harbor cottage.

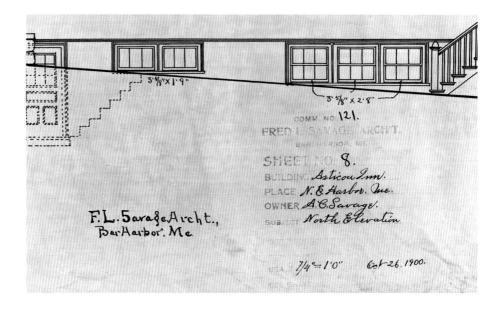

Mr. Fred L. Savage

Bar Harbor, Maine

Dear Sir:

As I understand it I can have my house to live in after a fashion on Tuesday next. I wish to have the furniture for my servants' rooms moved into the house on Monday next, and enough furniture for my daughters and my own rooms, on Tuesday. I wish to have the range and laundry stove put up on Monday, if possible, if not, on Tuesday morning.

I should like to have Mr. Kavanagh put up the shades on Saturday, if possible, certainly on Monday, in the third story, and my daughters and my own apartments. Also I want the fly screens put up on the third story windows on Saturday; on the basement windows on Monday; but not on the second or first floors until we are in the house, say on Wednesday. I wish all the screens on every window next week, doors and all.

In reference to the kitchen, I am anxious to have a little to say about the arrangement of drawers and cupboards. Mr. Orchard said there was no positive plan about the dresser that he knew. I wish a broom-closet, and I wish more small cupboards than I think are proposed. A good deal of space is needed for cooking utensils and pans. I send with this a little sketch which perhaps you can decipher, and which seems to me will be no more expensive to the builder nor consume any more time. If it can be done let me have it. I should think the space for the dresser is somewhere about seven feet, wide; then we should have three cupboards for cooking utensils, one near the sink, and two under the dresser. I should also like the blinds to be hung by Monday next. Will you please see that the hooks are put into the closets on third floor, also my daughters and my apartments. In my daughters the cleats on which the hooks are to be put are still as they were when the bars were taken off. I hope the hooks will be well chosen.

I should be glad to have the paper hanger go on with his work. The second coat of paint will be put on the morning room tomorrow: I should like the paper hung in that room. Friday and Saturday I should like the three small bedrooms on the second floor papered, if this can be done without delaying the work, otherwise: will you see to this and let me know so I can confer with Mr. Stuart tomorrow, as I have been so anxious not to have Mr.

Stuart leave the house until the entire second story and morning room are finished. Again referring to the kitchen, I am pleased with the plan of the cupboards with glass doors for dishes.

As I look at the house and our getting into it, I should suggest that the hall floor in the second story wait until Friday or Saturday to be finished, Saturday if possible; or, better still, could it not be finished better even as late as the lower floor hall is finished? Of necessity there will be much walking over for a few days next week, and it looks well enough as it is for us until the lower hall is to be finished. If this is satisfactory to the painters, I shall be pleased. Finish all the rooms of second story by Friday, but let the floor of hall wait until the following week.

Yours truly,

(signed) Agnes E. Platt

When Mrs. Platt's letter was transmitted to the contractor, somebody in Savage's office added a note below her signature: "Mr. Savage is out of town today, but he has asked me to make a copy of the above letter and send it to you so that you may see what Mrs. Platt wants and conform to her desires as far as possible."[11]

We do not know whether Agnes Platt was an unusually demanding client, but her letter indicates that Savage sometimes coordinated the work of contractors and craftsmen. The probate records of his estate show other facets of his professional life: he prepared and sold architectural plans, he ordered materials and tools (everything needed to produce buildings), he directed repairs and small projects for absentee owners, and he dealt with specialized contractors—masons, carpenters, plumbers, electricians, and painters—as work progressed.

During the six years of Savage's partnership with Stratton, the *Bar Harbor Record* mentioned seven new projects and five additions or alterations by Savage and Stratton (see Appendix). Throughout the partnership, Savage apparently continued to accept work as an individual, for the *Record* also credited him with two commissions without mentioning Stratton. The last news of the partnership was a notice (May 18, 1898) of their addition to the Moorings, the H. D. Gibson Cottage in Bar Harbor. On July 13, 1898, the *Record* announced that Stratton's design had been accepted for a new municipal hospital in Bar Harbor. Perhaps Stratton's success precipitated the dissolution of the partnership; after July 1898, they never worked together again. Except for newspaper records and drawings of the buildings they designed together, not much is known of their partnership.

Savage was extraordinarily productive, but we should remember those who helped him. He practiced architecture for thirty-six years (circa 1888–1924), and the partnership with Stratton covered six of those years. Newspaper references indicate that there was also a series of assistants in the office, apparently one at a time, for much of his career. His brother, George Augustus Savage (1873–1922), worked in his office during the winter of 1895–1896, but during most of their partnership, Savage and Stratton seem to have worked without assistants. Savage's next known assistant was Fred C. Watson, who was in the office during the fall and winter of 1905. In 1907, "Arthur Stanley, who has for some time been in the employ of F. L. Savage" left to take a job in Boston; that summer Stanley was replaced by Thurlow Workman. In 1913 another assistant, William G. Bunker, was judged competent to run the office in Savage's absence; as the *Bar Harbor Record* noted Bunker had already been in the office for four years at that time. Finally, the *Record* reported on December 15, 1915, that "Fred Savage has engaged the services of Mr. Louis E. Jackson, an architect from Boston, to assist him in his office. At present they are at work on a set of plans for an inn to replace the one that burned at Islesford, which it is hoped will be ready for the season of 1916."[12]

Louis E. Jackson (1878–circa 1932) was a Harvard graduate who had first worked in Washington, D.C., in the architectural office of Harry Vaughan, before he returned to Boston, where he was associated (1919–1924) with the firm of Parker, Thomas & Rice and with Guy Lowell.[13] If Jackson was hired specifically to help with the Islesford inn, he may only have been with Savage six or eight months. Whatever his tenure, he seems to have been the most experienced assistant, but the more obscure draftsmen should be remembered too, as their work helps explain Savage's prodigious output.

The Shingle Style

above and opposite: Hilltop Cottage,
Northeast Harbor, Fred L. Savage, 1888

Most of Savage's early work is in the shingle style, including his own house, whose entire exterior is shingled. The planar transitions from roof to porch to wall are sharply defined. There are no moldings, with shingles replacing traditional moldings and trim at the eaves, corners, and posts. Excepting the windows, the continuity of the shingled surface is unbroken. The dormers originally appeared (see page 63) through the lower slope of the gambrel roof, and a contrasting balcony appears as a void in the gable roof of the projecting end bay. Across the facade, a piazza and service porch create an unbroken band of shade. While Hilltop's facade presents many aspects of the shingle style, the interior plan, essentially balanced on either side of a modest entrance hall, is conservative (see page 65).

The shingle style is now accepted as part of the New England coastal landscape, but it was quite new when Savage designed his house. Scully, who defined the shingle style in 1949, was the first to perceive and articulate the emergence in the 1870s and 1880s of a new residential building type in which the extensive use of wooden shingles was one of several important characteristics.[14] He observed that the shingles often appeared to flow from roof to wall, over and around dormers and posts, as a thin, continuous plane or membrane. These shingled buildings, he noted, were usually asymmetrical in plan and elevation; they had extensive, sheltering porches and little classically derived exterior ornament. Architects working in the shingle style typically used free-flowing, informal interior plans and emphasized the natural qualities of their building materials. Taken together, these characteristics resulted in irregular shapes, textured surfaces, and pools of deep shade framed by local stone and weathered wooden shingles.[15]

Tracing the shingle style's complex historical roots, Scully found that H. H. Richardson (1838–1886), Stanford White (1853–1906), and other American architects, inspired by their English peers such as Richard Norman Shaw, Robert Kerr, and others, had combined Picturesque Medieval massing with the growing, pre-Centennial interest in vernacular, colonial American buildings. A new awareness of Japanese architecture and the legacy of Andrew Jackson Downing also contributed to the new mode. Scully demonstrated that early, partial manifestations of the shingle style began to appear in the 1870s, and he credited William Ralph Emerson's design for the C. J. Morrill cottage, Redwood, in Bar Harbor (1879) as the first wholly realized example of the shingle style.[16]

Emerson's peers appreciated his innovative use of shingles as well as his sculptural, free-flowing plans. In 1886 historian Maria G. van Rensselaer had observed that a

above and opposite: Redwood, Bar Harbor, William Ralph Emerson, 1879

house by Emerson "seems almost as much a part of nature's first intentions as do the rocks and trees themselves . . . its site and its surroundings seem to have been designed for its sole sake and service."[17] In the same vein, after his death in 1917, the Boston Society of Architects passed a resolution that called Emerson

> a native product of New England, delighting in ingenious contrivances and original inventions, filled with enthusiasms for whatever was spontaneous and natural, and abhorring conventions of every sort. He was the creator of the shingle country house of the New England coast, and taught his generation how to use local materials without apology, but rather with pride in their rough and homespun character.[18]

Intense interest in the shingle style lasted only about fifteen years (circa 1880–1895), but for that short period, Emerson, John Calvin Stevens and Albert Winslow Cobb of Portland, Maine; Bruce Price; McKim, Mead and White; and others pushed historical architectural conventions from the center stage along the New England coast. They replaced the accepted ornamental rhetoric with improvisations based on an inventive use of wood and stone. The anti-historical aspects of the shingle style were liberating, and with some imagination, asymmetrical shingle-style buildings along the shore can be viewed as being roughly analogous to the rocky shore with its dark mantle of spruce forest.

Although the shingle style is often called "natural" and "organic," Emerson's use of local materials is exceedingly unnatural. His work is obviously complex and artful and constantly calls attention to creative patterns and unanticipated shapes, shadows, and planes. In fact, Emerson's early reputation was based precisely on his ability to transform ordinary materials into ornament. His work in Bar Harbor, including Redwood, Mossley Hall (1885), Edgemere (1885), Thirlstane (1886), and the Briars (1890), offered young Savage a timely, concrete, and conveniently nearby lesson in the potential of the new mode.[19] Savage learned much from Emerson and his followers, but he would always tone things down in his own designs. He rarely used decoratively sawn shingles or laid the courses to form complex, geometric patterns, but with these exceptions, his early buildings incorporate the forms and characteristics we now associate with the shingle style. Savage's early work is often asymmetrical in plan and elevation, and the elevations are punctuated by both recessed and projecting porches,

balconies, and dormers. Even in modest cottages, he achieved a complex sense of massing and form by juxtaposing a variety of roof types, by creating pools of shadow within deep porches, and by using corner towers and turrets. Two details might be taken as hallmarks of his early shingle-style work. He often replaced the traditional extended, painted eaves with a single course of diagonally laid shingles. And more often than not, a main entrance designed by Savage, circa 1887–1900, was a Dutch door.

The shingle style was shaped by many influences, in which taste and social history play a major role, but practical and economic factors were part of the equation as well. First, shingled surfaces weather well. Unheated summerhouses in New England contract and expand as they freeze and thaw throughout the winter. This process opens seams between traditional clapboards and under and around turned and sawn wooden ornament. Shingles, however, overlap enough to accommodate movement without allowing moisture to penetrate. Secondly, New England shingles were typically made of rot-resistant white cedar and did not require the painting, caulking, attention, and expense needed to maintain traditional wooden sheathing and ornament. Thirdly, many steam-driven saws designed to make shingles were patented just before the Civil War. In 1855, for example, a British survey of American manufacturing reported "shingles, used for covering the roofs and sides of houses, are made in vast quantities. A circular saw cuts them . . . at the rate of from 7,000 to 10,000 per day, according to the nature of the wood."[20] In "1858 alone the United States Patent Office issued twenty patents for shingle machines and their parts."[21] Finally, the mass production of shingles provided an attractive market for small-diameter, second-growth timber. These

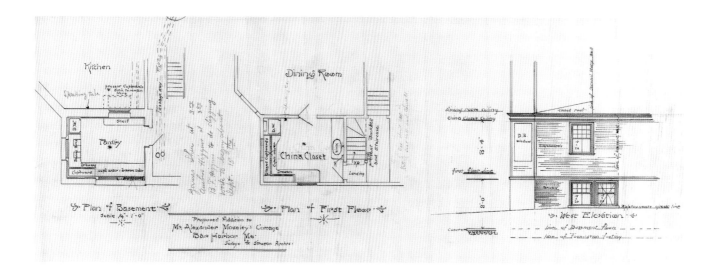

Kitchen

Pantry

⇒· Plan of Basement ·⇐
Scale ¼" 1'-0"

Dining Room

China Closet

⇒· Plan of First Floor ·⇐

West Elevation ·⇐

Proposed Addition to
Mr. Alexander Moseley's Cottage
Bar Harbor Me.
Savage & Simeon Archts.

Addition to Moseley Hall, Fred L. Savage, date unkown. Courtesy of the Northeast Harbor Library.

prosaic factors made shingles cheaply and readily available immediately after the Civil War, and this contributed to the creation and success of the shingle style.

Bar Harbor provided Savage with a convenient catalogue of approaches to seasonal residential design. The first cottage there is said to have been Birch Point (see p. 25), built in 1868 for Boston merchant Alpheus Hardy—its architect is unknown, but the builder was a Mr. Rider from Boston. The growth of Bar Harbor accelerated quickly after the Civil War, and local newspapers reported the construction of seventeen more cottages prior to 1875, thirty-five more between 1875 and 1880, and fifty-five more between 1880 and 1885, with an additional sixty-nine between 1885 and 1890. Local builders responded quickly, and the newspapers noted eleven Bar Harbor–based contractors at work on cottages prior to 1875.[22]

Watersmeet was the earliest Bar Harbor cottage that can be assigned to a specific architect. It was designed by C. C. Haight, a New York architect, for Governor Morris Ogden in 1873. In 1887 Watersmeet was remodeled by DeGrass Fox for George Washington Vanderbilt. Vanderbilt renamed the cottage Point D'Acadie and had A. W. Longfellow of Boston design two cottages nearby—Whileaway (1901) for Mrs. J. B. Trevor and Islescote (1901–02) for Mrs. W. J. Schiefflin, one of his nieces. Savage served as superintending, or on-site, architect for Islescote.

In the mid-1870s a group of architects from Maine began to practice in Bar Harbor (W. A. Jordan, George W. Orff, George Rich, John E. Clark, and Henry Richards), but by the end of the decade, most of the major commissions were being awarded to architects from Boston and New York. In addition to William Ralph Emerson, who ultimately designed twenty-one cottages on Mount Desert, Bruce Price from New York designed nine, Rotch and Tilden from Boston designed twenty, Andrews, Jacques & Rantoul of Boston designed twenty-five, Ware and Van Brunt from Boston designed two, and Henry W. Hartwell, also from Boston, designed two. During the period from 1888 to 1924, Fred Savage would design at least three hundred buildings in Bar Harbor and environs. He also supervised construction or designed additions or alterations for another twelve buildings that had been designed by others.[23]

top: Moseley Hall, Bar Harbor, William
Ralph Emerson, 1883. Courtesy of the Bar
Harbor Historical Society.

bottom: Point D'Acadie, Bar Harbor,
Charles Coolidge Haight, 1869; remodeled by DeGrass Fox, 1889. Courtesy of
the Bar Harbor Historical Society.

Savage's Early Work in
Northeast Harbor

The Morris Cottage (1889)
and the Phillips Cottage (1889–1890)

The development of summer cottages in Northeast Harbor did not begin in earnest until the late 1880s, about a decade after the same phenomenon in Bar Harbor. Fred Savage started his career by designing cottages for people who had purchased lots from his father, who owned approximately three hundred acres along the eastern shore of Northeast Harbor. In her memoirs, Reynolds remembers playing in the woods above Asticou and finding "look-outs . . . tall towers with stairs leading for forty feet or so to a square platform above where we could see the view of the harbor." She assumed that A. C. Savage built the towers "to show the view to prospective buyers."[24]

One of Savage's early commissions was a shingle-style cottage for Dr. Caspar Morris of Philadelphia (1858–1944), who was the chief medical examiner of the Reading Railroad and a professor of clinical medicine at the Philadelphia Polyclinic College.[25] The Morris cottage was built in 1889 above the Asticou Inn and was called by the local press "Dr. Morris's Chalet."[26] The reference to a Swiss chalet was probably prompted by the cottage's siting on the side of a hill with its facade and porch facing downhill, supported by posts above the sloping land. This is the siting a popular American architectural writer described as a main characteristic of the chalet style:

> Its principle feature is the verandah or gallery, covered by the projecting roof, and supported by the open framework. This is at once bold and simple, suggestive of summer enjoyment and of winter protection. . . . Circumstances similar to those which make this style proper on the Alpine slopes often exist among us, and it is for some such position that the design is intended. It would suit well the southern slope of some steep and rugged hill.[27]

Beyond siting, the Morris Cottage and the conceptually similar Phillips Cottage that Savage designed nearby for his brother-in-law Frederick I. Phillips, do not resemble chalet-inspired houses then being built in America; they lack the decoratively sawn trim—balustrades, eaves, and brackets—that Downing and the English writer P. F. Robinson popularized as "Swiss." Nonetheless, the reporter's loose use of the term is useful, for it points to the interest in international styles that influenced Savage and the development of Mount Desert.

A fascination with foreign and historic styles has been a recurring theme in American architecture. Every generation since the 1830s has produced advocates of a uniquely national expression in the arts, but most American creators, including Savage,

Morris Cottage, Northeast Harbor,
Fred L. Savage, 1889

above and opposite: Morris Cottage

above and opposite: Phillips Cottage, Northeast Harbor, Fred L. Savage, 1889–1890

have used the past as a reservoir of ideas. To understand his career, we must keep in mind Savage's acceptance of historic and foreign styles as well as the background of his clients. The people who commissioned summer cottages on Mount Desert were typically educated and affluent. They favored styles as "worldly" as themselves, and most of them did not identify with local architectural traditions.

An interest in foreign styles and places is a common element in descriptions of early tourism on Mount Desert. One of the first commentators, journalist Clara Barnes Martin, described the Rodick Hotel's new bathing facilities (hot or cold, salt or fresh water) noting that she was not describing "Stamboul nor Damascus." She likened a new cottage in Bar Harbor to "a Como Villa, just on the edge of an overhanging terrace" and mentioned that another cottage was "in Swiss style," and

> as I look up from my table, I behold on the walls of my chalet bits of Italy, Venice and Japan, but neither Vesuvius, the Apennines nor Fusiami can frame a sweeter, lovelier picture than that which opens from my window. Frenchman's Bay lies before me like a wonderful inland lake. . . . No one can leave here without vowing to return. Like the fountain of Trevi, drink of its cooling draughts and the spell which binds you to the place can never be broken.[28]

B. F. DeCosta, an Episcopal clergyman from Massachusetts who wrote extensively on American history, writing five years later, contrasted Mount Desert favorably with "the coast-scenery of Cornwall, the Isle of Wight, and the Mediterranean," while *Chisholm's Mount-Desert Guide-Book* (1888) described the seaward view from Bar Harbor as a "great Scottish loch [looking] toward the Hebrides" and noted the "Corniche Road, perhaps the finest drive on the island . . . from Duck Brook to Hull's Cove" with its "*chateaux en Maine*" including "Sonogee, the Swiss chalet of E. C. Haight."[29] Late-nineteenth-century Americans often accepted European culture as a gauge of beauty and sophistication, and it is not surprising that their architects aimed to give form to these aspirations.

Harborside (1890–1895)

Fred Savage's first major project was Harborside, a development at the head of Northeast Harbor consisting of a communal dining building and seven houses. He drew a site plan of the buildings for the developer James Terry Gardiner (1842–1912) and his partner, whom we only know as Frank, or William, Wiswell,[30] and designed the communal building and cottages (Aerie, Isis, Grey Pine, Sweet Briar, Wagstaff, and Fermata) in 1890.[31] George Soulis of Northeast Harbor was the general contractor for Harborside, and he completed the first seven buildings by 1893. Journey's End, the final cottage, designed for Dr. and Mrs. Joseph Tunis of Philadelphia, was finished by 1895. Mrs. Tunis's brother was Frank Furness (1839–1912), a prominent Philadelphian architect, and according to family tradition, Savage used Furness's plans to develop the construction drawings.[32]

The Harborside complex was the first major development by outsiders in Northeast Harbor. Its shingle-style inn provided convenient, communal dining, but the complex was not meant to function as a traditional hotel. Rather, Gardiner and Wiswell defined their principal market as affluent families who might rent by the month or season or buy the cottages; the individual houses were therefore set on separate lots, each with shore frontage. Savage designed the houses as harmonious neighbors with compatible setbacks from the street and similar side yards. The street facades are private and pleasant, demonstrating the freedom, variety, and informality characteristic of the shingle style. Details and massing vary from house to house. Invariably, however, covered porches and open piazzas dominate the rear elevations facing the water view.[33]

We often take these open rear facades for granted—they seem so logical—but they are a principal characteristic and contribution of the shingle style. The prominence given porches by Savage and his peers was a post–Civil War phenomenon that was a concrete, architectural expression of the growing aesthetic response to nature. Like most architects working on Mount Desert from around 1880 to 1920, Savage emphasized porches and piazzas because he knew that the rusticators wanted to be outdoors. The early summer people rarely wrote specifically about the houses, but they nostalgically recalled time on the water or mountainsides, so architectural features leading into the landscape were clearly appropriate.

The relationship among the Harborside buildings is significant. In the earlier development of hotels with cottages at Bar Harbor and Northeast Harbor such as the Asticou Inn and the Rockend Hotel, the communal buildings were always primary and the cottages secondary. This relationship was reversed at Harborside, where the

above: Harborside, Northeast Harbor,
Fred L. Savage, 1890

following spread, left page: Isis, Northeast
Harbor, Fred L. Savage, 1890

following spread, right page: Fermata,
Northeast Harbor, Fred L. Savage, 1890

Fermata, Northeast Harbor,
Fred L. Savage, 1890

cottages occupied the shore, had the best views, and provided a significant measure of privacy. Architecturally, Harborside thus foreshadowed the nature of development in Northeast Harbor as a community catering to long-term, seasonal residents living in cottages rather than hotels. Harborside also provided a launching pad for Savage's career as a designer of large summer cottages.

Local historians have pointed out that the early summer guests in Northeast Harbor influenced the community and helped create a setting and experience quite different from the larger, more transient and bustling Bar Harbor by building isolated cottages for themselves. The founders of the Northeast Harbor summer colony, President Eliot, Bishop Doane, and Joseph Henry Curtis, started this trend, and Savage later designed similar houses for some of their children. Gardiner, however, directly affected the whole community by playing a prominent role in the creation of Harborside. He was later also involved in creating important roads in Northeast Harbor, such as Sargeant Drive and Peabody Drive, and in establishing the Northeast Harbor Water Company and the Northeast Harbor Village Improvement Society.

Gardiner was a civil engineer who had worked from coast to coast before settling in Maine. Immediately prior to coming to Northeast Harbor for the first time in the summer of 1880 as the fiancé of Eliza Greene Doane, Bishop Doane's daughter, he had been surveying a proposed joint Canadian-American park at Niagara Falls with Frederick Law Olmsted (the public access and park on the American side of the falls was shaped by their work).[34] Before that, in 1864, Gardiner had worked as a military engineer with Clarence King under Olmsted's direction, preparing surveys in California that defined the area subsequently preserved as Yosemite Valley and Mariposa Big Tree Grove. After the Civil War he continued to work on geological surveys of California and other states. For a decade (1876–1886) he directed the survey of New York State while simultaneously serving as a member of the state board of health and a consulting engineer to various railroads.[35] Clearly able and energetic, he was also president of the Street Railroad & Lighting Company of St. Joseph, Missouri (1892–1895) and was elected president of the Mexican Coke & Coal Company in 1899.[36]

Gardiner's experience as an engineer and administrator was influential in his development of Northeast Harbor and its environs. Working with Olmsted inevitably developed or honed his appreciation for the value—in every sense of the word—of natural vistas. He first visited Niagara with Olmsted on May 28, 1879, and wrote that "after careful study of the ground, Mr. Olmsted and I are of [the] opinion" that the

Aerie, Northeast Harbor,
Fred L. Savage, 1890

above: Sweet Briar, Northeast Harbor,
Fred L. Savage, 1890

opposite: Aerie, Northeast Harbor,
Fred L. Savage, 1890

above and opposite: Journey's End,
Northeast Harbor, Fred L. Savage, 1890

above and opposite: Ye Haven, Northeast Harbor, attributed to John E. Clark, 1885

scenic value of the falls had been compromised and would soon be ruined by commercial encroachment, that the state should acquire the shoreline, demolish the buildings, and provide and preserve public access.[37] Gardiner would face a similar situation in Northeast Harbor. Working with the Village Improvement Society, he unsuccessfully tried several times to move the commercial district uphill, away from the shore. By siting all of the houses uphill near the road, the Harborside plan preserves the view of the shoreline and harbor as an amenity shared by everyone using the houses. Savage's plan probably reflects Gardiner, as a knowledgeable client, working harmoniously with an able and understanding architect.

On the western headland at the entrance to Northeast Harbor, Gardiner built a cottage for his own family, which he called Ye Haven (1883–1885). It was apparently designed by John E. Clark of Bar Harbor,[38] but according to local tradition, Savage participated in some of the early alterations and additions to Ye Haven; the service wing, bay windows, and piazza are characteristic of his work in the shingle style.

The Northeast Harbor
Reading Room (1891–1892)

Construction at Gardiner's Harborside began in 1890 and continued for several years. While it was under way, in 1891, Savage designed the shingle-style Northeast Harbor Reading Room. This library was a private club where members of the summer colony could "house their books and . . . meet and read their magazines."[39] It was organized during the summer of 1890 by President Gilman of John Hopkins University, who formed an association and purchased a lot from Herman Savage, owner of the nearby Rockend Hotel. Fred Savage designed the building with three rooms—a book room, a writing room, and a periodical room—and it was complete and in service during the summer of 1892.

The Reading Room is a one-story building with a hipped roof that extends without a break over a porch or piazza across the whole facade. The entire exterior is shingled and shows no extraneous ornament. Windowsills are set at shoulder height on the side and rear walls to accommodate bookshelves and desks beneath them. Judging from old photographs, the interior was Spartan, wholly dedicated to reading and writing. Architecturally and institutionally, the Reading Room reflected the value that leaders of the summer colony placed on cultivating the mind. Daniel Coit Gilman, who initiated the library, first came to Northeast Harbor in the summer of 1885 to visit President Eliot. The following summer, his family spent the summer in "a little hotel in Northeast Harbor" and

> a custom arose of Mr. Gilman reading aloud for an hour after breakfast. It was most informal, a dozen persons sometimes sharing with the family the pleasure of hearing some book of history or travel, which Mr. Gilman had chosen with care before leaving home.[40]

The Reading Room Association permitted the public to use their library, and Herman Savage called it a civic asset in an advertisement for his nearby Rockend Hotel.[41] Public use of the Reading Room potentially brought everyone in Northeast Harbor into contact with Fred Savage's work. The building served as a Reading Room until 1950 when a new library was built, and the Reading Room was converted into a summer cottage.

Reading Room, Northeast Harbor,
Fred L. Savage, 1891

Overedge (1896), *Brackenfell* (1896), and Other Early Shingle-Style Cottages (1886–1899)

above and opposite: Overedge, Northeast Harbor, Fred L. Savage, 1896

President Gilman must have been satisfied with Savage's work on the Reading Room, for he subsequently commissioned the architect to design Overedge, a large shingle-style cottage on the harbor. Overedge is aptly named. Sited on the lip of the steep, rocky shore, the design is notable for its porches and balconies that overlook the harbor. Like many of Savage's "outdoor rooms," these porches simultaneously flood the interior with light and provide vistas that contrast the urbane, well-organized comforts of the household with the ever-changing panorama of light and water, and wind and tide.

The *Boston Transcript* reported on June 24, 1896, that "the western half of Mt. Desert continues to gain in popularity as the summer resort of college presidents.... At Northeast Harbor, President Gilman of Hopkins, after having been a boarder from many years, has lately become a houseowner.... At Asticou (formerly known as 'Savage's'), President C. K. Adams, late of Cornell, but now of Wisconsin University, will this year occupy the house built from him the past season."[42] President Adams's shingle-style cottage, Brackenfell, was sited on the ridge above Harborside, and it too was designed by Savage. Mature spruce trees now surround the house and largely block the original view of the harbor. The house is approached from below by a circuitous drive, which gives visitors a chance to admire the pink granite foundations and generous porches wrapping around the shingled facade. The entrance is on the uphill side tucked between two projecting bays, which vary in form and detail. At Brackenfell Savage combined Tudor revival half-timbering and stucco in the gables with the flared overhangs, asymmetry, and porches of the shingle style. The entrance hall contains a staircase and doorways into the living room on the left and a smoking room and dining room on the right. Directly in front of the entrance, adjacent the staircase, is a window seat, designed as a place to sit and savor the harbor view.

Following Harborside, much of Savage's early work consisted of summer cottages in the shingle style. In addition to Overedge and Brackenfell, notable early examples in Northeast Harbor and environs include Grasslands (1886) for Samuel Duncan Sargent; L'Escale (1890) for Benjamin W. Arnold; Rosserne (1891) for Rev. Cornilius B. Smith; The Ledge for W. W. Vaughn and Birchcroft for Carrol S. Tyson (both in 1892); Ledge Lawn (1895) for Miss Francis Clark; the Alders (now called Over the Way) for Samuel Duncan Sargeant and Ravensthorp on Greenings Island for James G. Thorp (both in 1896); Hilltop Cottage (1897) for Samuel A. Eliot; and Treetops for Rev. William Adams Brown and the Scull Cottage for Gidieon Scull (both in 1899).

above and opposite: Overedge

above and opposite: Brackenfell,
Northeast Harbor, Fred L. Savage, 1896

Savage's early shingle-style houses demonstrate several types of interior plans
that he tended to adapt and reuse to suit the circumstances. For the smallest commissions, such as the Morris Cottage or the Reading Room, a piazza or porch across the
facade provided access to the main entrance that opened directly into a living room. In
small buildings he avoided the use of halls, so that doors opened from the living room
directly into a flanking dining room and a kitchen and sometimes bedrooms in the rear
of the house. For larger houses with dramatic views, he often used a long, narrow rectangular plan. Houses of this type, including the Eliot Cottage, the Scull Cottage,
Brackenfell, Ravensthorp, and later the Williamson cottage at Dark Harbor and
Highseas near Bar Harbor, were invariably sited perpendicular to the view. The
principal entry was usually on the inland or uphill side so that the building obscured
the view as one approached. The main entrance led into an open, hublike center where
the principal staircase and doorways to the kitchen and dining rooms joined the broad
opening to a large, rectangular living area. Windows and French doors opposite the
entry flooded the area with light and framed glimpses of the porches and the view
beyond. The living area (to the left of the entry at Hilltop and Brackenfell) was strongly
defined by dark, linear beams and moldings. The high point of this room was typically
a large masonry chimney breast and fireplace—made of rough fieldstone and cobbles at
Brackenfell, Hilltop, and Devilstone.

Many features that reoccur in Savage's shingle-style work were part of a design
vocabulary that he shared with his contemporaries. Just as surely as Savage's work was
influenced by the topography, it was influenced by other architects as well. Westover,

above and opposite: Brackenfell

for example, perched atop School House Ledge above Northeast Harbor, was designed by William Price (1861–1916), known for his role in the arts-and-crafts movement, for Susan English in 1902. Its porches, gambrel roof, and beamed interior give us a glimpse of the context in which Savage was working.

The largest homes designed by Savage tend to have complex asymmetrical plans, usually at least two rooms deep. Recurring features include a large butler's pantry between kitchen and dining room, a complex staircase adjacent the principal entry, and piazzas and porches along the facade opposite the entrance. Throughout his career, Savage used gambrel roofs, a variety of types of dormers and eyebrow windows, projecting bay windows, and recessed balconies and colonial revival ornament such as Palladian windows, lathe-turned balusters, and columns to accent shingled elevations. Like his mentors Peabody and Stearns, he reveled in variety, and unexpected details often make his work appealing—the dormer of the Rockend Colonial, also known as the Yellow House, which he designed for his brother Herman in 1885, and the balcony at Birchcroft, designed in 1892 for Carrol S. Tyson, make this point effectively.

above and opposite: Ledgelawn, also
known as the Clark Cottage, Northeast
Harbor, Fred L. Savage, 1895–1897

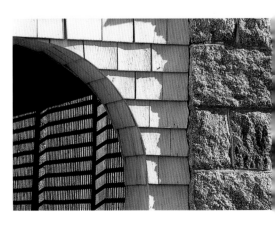

above and opposite: L'Escale, Northeast
Harbor, Fred L. Savage, 1890

above and opposite: Treetops, Seal
Harbor, Fred L. Savage, 1899

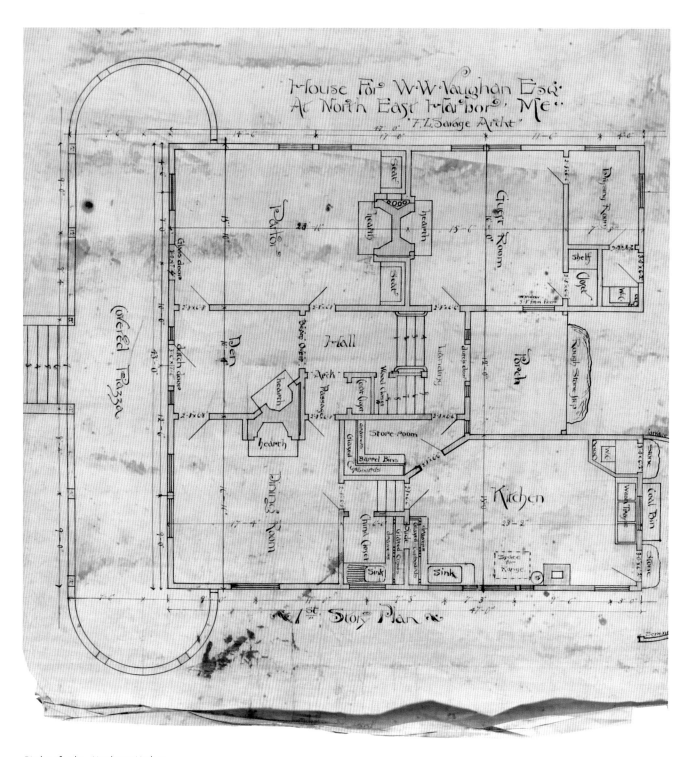

Birchcroft, plan, Northeast Harbor,
Fred L. Savage, 1892. Courtesy of the
Northeast Library.

top: Birchcroft

bottom: Birchcroft, south elevation,
Courtesy of the Northeast Library.

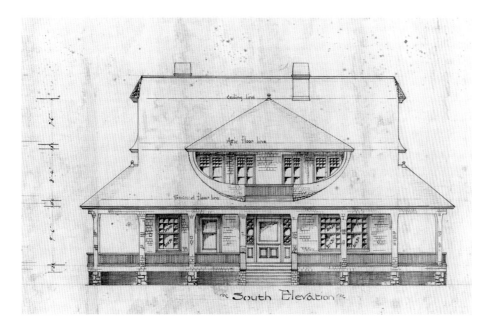

Westover, Northeast Harbor,
William Price, 1902

top and following spread: Westover

bottom: Ravensthorpe, north elevation,
Greenings Island, Fred L. Savage, 1896.
Courtesy of the Northeast Harbor Library.

The Ledge, Northeast Harbor,
Fred L. Savage, 1892

Rockend Colonial, Northeast Harbor,
Fred L. Savage, 1895

The Rosserne Cottage

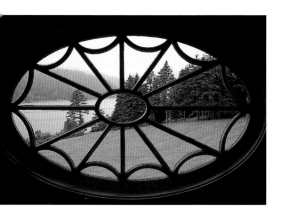

above and opposite: Rosserne, Northeast Harbor, Fred L. Savage, 1891

Rosserne, built for Rev. Dr. Cornelius Bishop Smith from New York, is Savage's most complex shingle-style cottage on Mount Desert. Rev. Smith was the first summer resident to move up Somes Sound, two miles around the shore from the village.

Rosserne is sited on the sloping eastern shore of Somes Sound, and many exterior features make it memorable. Its main entrance is on the eastern, or inland, facade, where planes of shingles sheathe the gambrel roof, walls, exterior staircase, and the round corner porch and turret with its bell-like ogee roof. The cottage's elevations are punctuated by a strong pattern of shadow. Curves appear playfully everywhere—in the round arches over the stair and service porch and recessed entry, beneath the bay window, in the flared base of the overhanging second story, and in the plan and silhouette of the corner turret. Porches and balconies on the western side of the house offer a view of the sunset over the Sound and catch the prevailing summer breeze from the southwest.

Mrs. Lincoln Cromwell, Rev. Smith's daughter, wrote of childhood summers at Rosserne, nostalgically remembering time spent outside enjoying the beautiful landscape:

> I begin with an old felt hat, by sun and storm turned to a marvelous orange
> rust color, for in our first summer here we saw that hat more than anything
> else silhouetted against the sky, because we were sailing day after day
> with Captain Walls. . . . The Harbor was full of rowboats, canoes and sail-
> boats, . . . and we communicated with each other almost entirely by water. Our
> days were spent on the water except when we climbed mountains or took
> excursions on a buckboard for nine with Blackie and Gold Dust as our
> steeds. . . . Many people wonder just what it is that makes this place unique
> and creates the devotion of so many people. It may be partly explained, first,
> by the beauty of the Island. Second, by the cool weather and many sports with
> simple, appropriate equipment. Third, by our Sundays containing church
> services, swimming, family dinner, climbs or sails, and Sunset Services.[43]

Rev. Smith invited neighbors to participate in these services, and for many people the Sunset Services on the grounds of Rosserne became a meaningful part of the rhythm of summer. Friends, young and old, gathered outdoors near the sunset-gilt water with darkening mountains on the far shore silhouetted against the sky. These services and the setting must have evoked the same inspirational reveries that had drawn landscape painters to Mount Desert half a century earlier.

above and opposite: Rosserne, elevations and floor plan. Courtesy of the Northeast Harbor Library.

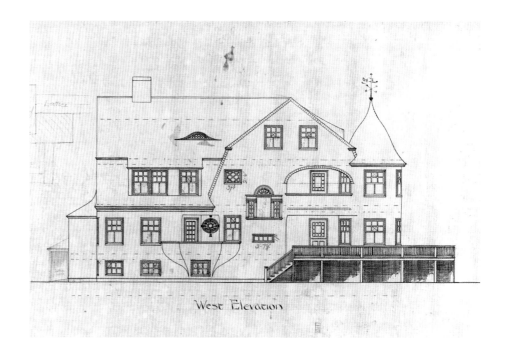

West Elevation

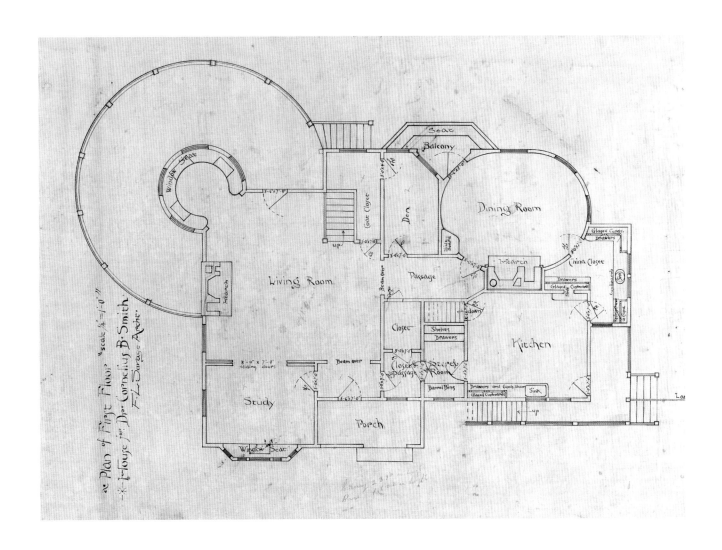

A Plan of First Floor. scale ¼"=1'-0"
House for Cornelius B. Smith
F. L. Savage Archt.

Living Room

Study

Window Seat

Window Seat

Fireplace

Porch

Closet
Passage

Closet

Shelves
Drawers

Barrel Bins

Secret Room

Kitchen

Sink

Drawers and Cupds. Under
(Glazed Cupboards)

Drawers
Glazed Cupboard

Glazed Cupds.
Drawers

China Closet

Cupboards

Passage

Hearth

Den

Coat Closet

up

Balcony

Seat

Dining Room

123

above and opposite: Rosserne

above: View from the grounds
of Rosserne

opposite: Rosserne

Stylistic Diversity

While his reputation was growing among the rusticators, Savage was also accepting commissions from year-round, local residents, and he worked successfully for both groups throughout his career. His designs for summer people usually reflect one or another of the styles popular in New England at the time, such as the shingle style. By contrast, his local commissions typically represent conservative, vernacular traditions. The diversity of his clientele and the array of styles he used suggest that Savage was socially adept and pragmatic and flexible, rather than doctrinaire, in matters of design.

His work for local clients includes the Dirigo Theater for Robert P. King in Ellsworth; the Picture Theater for Byron H. Mayo & Son in Southwest Harbor; alterations to the Star Theater in Bar Harbor; alterations to the N. Hillson & Son store and the Green Brothers store, both in Bar Harbor; a store for Hamor and Stanley Heating and Plumbing in Northeast Harbor; a garage for the Bangor Motor Company in Bangor; the commercial William Ward Building in Manset; and alterations for the Mt. Block Company Building (now occupied by the Bar Harbor Banking and Trust) in Bar Harbor. Renovations and additions to the Manchester family's Old Homestead exemplify Savage's approach to the vernacular.

Old Homestead, Northeast Harbor,
additions by Fred L. Savage, ca. 1900

The Old Homestead (additions and alterations, circa 1900)

above and opposite: Old Homestead, Northeast Harbor, additions by Fred L. Savage, ca. 1900

John Manchester had settled on Manchester's Point, the Somes Sound side of Northeast Harbor, around 1775. One of his sons, Major John Manchester, built a New England Cape Cod dwelling there in 1820, and here Fred Savage's mother, Emily Manchester, was born in 1835.[44] The Old Homestead was moved to its present location during the nineteenth century. Although the date is uncertain, it is clear that Savage prepared alterations and additions to the cottage consisting of a two-story service wing angling back from the north side of the existing house. The work was done for Abram Gilpatrick, fisherman, farmer, sailor, kinsman, and year-round resident, but it provided the same functional amenities that Savage was designing for the rusticators. The new wing joined the house at the dining room, adjacent to which Savage placed a butler's pantry and a separate cook's pantry. Beyond the pantries were a large kitchen and a servants' hall and porch. A bathroom and three bedrooms occupied the second floor of the new wing. The new dormers, windows, wooden siding and trim matched the existing house and barn.

At the Manchester Homestead, Savage was working within well-established traditions, for the Cape Cod dwelling with a connected woodshed, ell, and barn is among the quintessential vernacular architectural forms throughout northern New England. Wherever these linked-together buildings are found, the coupling of their discrete components suggests an interrelated, organic function as clearly as the exoskeleton of an insect. Savage rarely used self-consciously stylistic ornament when he was working with vernacular forms; his ability to satisfy the diverse tastes of the summer people and local residents was one of the keys to his success.

Reverie Cove (1892)

above and opposite: Reverie Cove, Bar Harbor, Fred L. Savage, 1892

The work at the Manchester Homestead represents Savage's response to local, traditional forms. Reverie Cove (1892), on the other hand, shows how quickly and thoroughly he embraced the historical revival styles. Reverie Cove was Savage's first major Bar Harbor cottage, and he published it in the *Scientific American Building Monthly*. It was designed for Mrs. John Davies Jones of Washington, D.C., "in the Spanish style, and its exterior walls are built of stucco, which is stained a soft yellow color while the trimmings are painted an apple green. The shingle roof is stained a brilliant red and forms a very happy contrast with the color scheme."[45] Several aspects of the design must have made Savage describe it as "Spanish." Perhaps he meant for the red roof to evoke ceramic tiles and the stuccoed walls to suggest adobe. The large, widely spaced brackets beneath the overhangs may have reminded him of the ends of rafters protruding through the walls of Spanish colonial buildings. The central axis of the facade is a large triple window within a round arch, and perhaps he considered this arch and the geometric panel beneath it Spanish. In any case, the composition represents a marked departure from his earlier work. Reverie Cove is sited on the shore, and its dark interior provides a restful contrast to the glaring light on the water. Savage described the entrance vestibule and living hall as being "painted in dark Flemish oak." The living hall had "a paneled wainscoting and a beamed ceiling," a complex staircase that was silhouetted against latticed windows, and a fireplace "built of old gold Roman brick." The Reverie Cove interior plan foreshadows plans he would develop for other major cottages. The entrance—and this is typical of his shore cottages—is on the facade opposite the water. Entering, you face the light and glimpse porches and the sea beyond. At Reverie Cove the smoking room or study is adjacent the vestibule; the large entry hall is balanced by the staircase to the left of the vestibule and the fireplace on the opposite, or seaward, wall. A dining room and parlor open off of the entrance hall.[46]

above and opposite: Reverie Cove, Bar
Harbor, Fred L. Savage, 1892. *Scientific
American Building Monthly* (December,
1904), 120 and 121. Courtesy of the
Northeast Harbor Library.

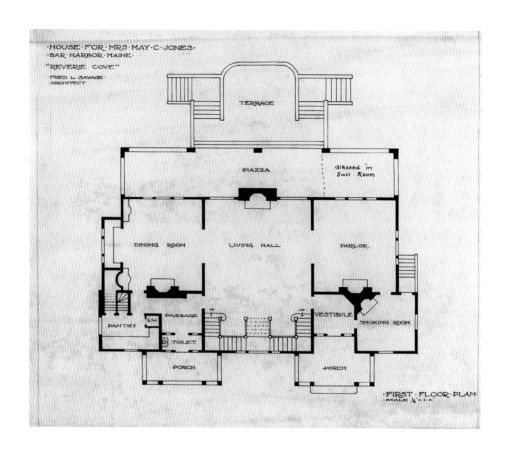

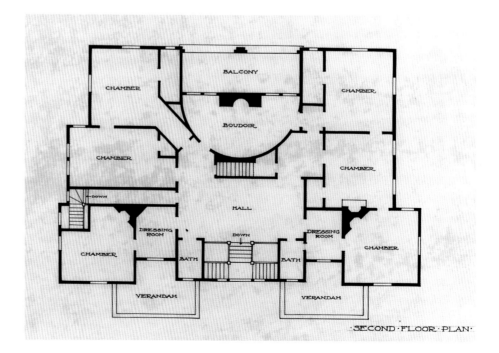

above: Reverie Cove

opposite: Reverie Cove, floor plans.
Courtesy of the Mount Desert Island
Historical Society.

above and opposite: Reverie Cove

The Islesboro Cottages (1894–1916)

As Savage's reputation spread, so did his commissions, and by the mid-1890s he, in partnership with Stratton as well as working alone, began to design summer cottages beyond Mount Desert in the new, growing colony on Islesboro in western Penobscot Bay. Summer development there had begun in 1868 with the construction of a seasonal boarding house at Ryder's Cove, and during the next seventeen years a number of small cottages were built by people from nearby Bangor. The development gathered speed when in 1884, James Murray Howe, an entrepreneur from Boston who was involved in the development of North Haven, visited Islesboro. The next year he brought the Philadelphian developer James D. Winsor, who formed the Islesboro Land and Improvement Company in 1888. The following year the company erected a thirty-nine-room inn and wharf in Dark Harbor, Islesboro, and began selling lots. The development was quickly successful. Fourteen large cottages were built between 1891 and 1897, and at least forty more were built during the next five years.[47]

Savage designed far more of the Islesboro cottages than any of his peers. Savage and Stratton worked on four cottages between 1894 and 1898. Subsequently, working alone, Savage designed nine more between 1898 and 1916. By comparison, Peabody and Stearns designed four cottages on Islesboro between 1898 and 1903; Evans, Warner & Register of Philadelphia had three Islesboro commissions between 1912 and 1917; and John LaValle of Boston also designed three cottages there between 1898 and 1900. Many other architects and firms had one or two commissions apiece. Earle G. Shettleworth's list of those who designed one or two cottages on Islesboro includes Lewis C. Albro, Mott B. Schmitt, and William A. Delano of New York; and William T. Aldrich, Francis R. Allen, Frank Chouteau Brown, Guy Lowell, Eliot T. Putnam, William G. Rantoul, and Edmund M. Wheelwright from Boston. Most architects who worked on Islesboro during the construction boom—like most of the clients—came from Philadelphia. They included Bissell, Sinkler & Tilden; Cope & Stewardson; Wilson Eyre; Mellor, Meigs & Howe; Stewardson & Page; Tilden & Register; and Zantzinger, Borie & Medary.[48]

Several of the cottages Savage designed on Islesboro resembled his early shingle-style projects in Northeast Harbor, but much of his work there reflected the larger scale and stylistic diversity that marked his later career in Bar Harbor (circa 1895–1924). Dark Harbor was settled mainly by wealthy financiers, industrialists, and their families who showed little interest in the architectural understatement found in Northeast Harbor; consequently, on Islesboro Savage quickly showed his ability to create cottages in a range of current styles. Between 1894 and 1900 he was responsible for three Islesboro cottages in the shingle style (the Paul B. Valle cottage, 1896; the William H. Draper cottage, 1899; the Charles Platt, Jr., cottage, 1900); he designed two more that combined the shingle style with colonial revival ornament (the Ella Williamson cottage, 1894–1895; the Charles Platt, Sr., cottage, 1898–1899) and another two using Tudor revival features with the shingle style (the George S. Silsbee cottage, 1898–1899; the Alexander Biddle cottage, 1902–1903). He also designed three large, purely colonial revival cottages on Islesboro (the William Prall–Harold I. Pratt cottage, 1897–1898, and the George Philler cottage, 1895–1896, both of which were designed with Stratton; and the Mrs. John W. Minturn cottage, 1898–1899). As Peabody and Stearns had done, Savage used styles interchangeably like clothing, tailoring plans to suit his clients' taste.

Beyond his ability as a designer, Savage was successful on Islesboro because he knew the contractors, craftsmen, and sources of materials. Architects based elsewhere could not match his local knowledge or his ability to provide on-site supervision. Moreover, repeated commissions from clients' families and from successive owners indicate that he clearly had a reputation for efficiency and fairness. For example, having designed a shingle-style cottage for Charles Platt, Sr., of Philadelphia, in 1898, Savage was hired again to add a round corner porch similar to that of Rosserne's in 1900. While he was working on this addition he created another shingle-style cottage nearby for Charles Platt, Jr. Another example is the large (128 by 45 feet) colonial revival cottage he designed for the Rev. Dr. William Prall in 1898. Thirteen years later Prall sold the cottage to Harold I. Pratt, and the new owner retained Savage to design an addition consisting of twenty-one rooms and six baths. Construction time for his Islesboro cottages was typically only nine or ten months from start to finish. The Biddle; Draper; Minturn; Philler; Platt, Sr.; Platt, Jr.; Prall; and Silsbee cottages were all begun in the fall and ready for occupancy the following summer. The builders Savage worked with were mostly local, and many contractors and craftsmen came from nearby towns. They boarded on Islesboro and worked twelve hours a day, six days a week. Lumber and millwork came largely from the mills in Bangor.[49]

The Williamson Cottage (1894–1895)

Bragdon Cottage, Northeast Harbor,
Fred L. Savage, 1898

The Ella Williamson cottage was Savage's first major commission on Islesboro. It clearly demonstrates his ability to combine the three-dimensional, sculptural freedom of the shingle style with the crisp definition of colonial revival ornament. The cottage must have been under construction by the winter of 1894–1895, for on May 31, 1895, the *Industrial Journal* of Bangor reported that "Geo. H. Wilbur, the Foxcroft contractor, has returned from Dark Harbor, Islesboro, where he had the contract for the mason work for the elegant cottage just built for Miss Ella Williamson of New York. F. L. Savage of Bar Harbor is the architect and D. J. Manchester of Northeast Harbor did the wood work."[50] Any details that remained to be done must have gone smoothly, as the same newspaper reported on July 4, 1895, that "Miss Williamson has her cottage at Dark Harbor all completed and furnished in superb style and has moved in."[51]

The plan of the Williamson house is compact with one-and-a-half stories tucked beneath a cross-axial gambrel roof. The shorter, central axis contains the entrance, principal staircase, and reception hall. Service areas (kitchen, pantry, laundry, service stairs, porch, and entrance) are to the left, and the library is to the right of the main entrance. The basic footprint is a rectangle set parallel to the water with a veranda breaking forward toward the shore. The plan and elevation both contain features that reoccur in Savage's work: As at the Bragdon cottage (1898) in Northeast Harbor, the principal entrance is tucked away around a corner within the shadow of the overhanging gambrel roof and second story. Here Savage uses the baroque strategies of juxtaposing a sense of spatial constriction and expansion and forcing a sudden change of perspective. The entrance leads into a small vestibule, while immediately to the visitor's right is a large reception hall providing access to the whole first floor and views beyond the piazzas.

The prominence given the reception hall in the Williamson cottage plan was a hallmark of modernity. Van Rensselaer observed in 1886 that for

> a long time the most usual pattern in our country homes [was to] build a rectangular box with a straight 'entry' through the middle and two square rooms on each hand. If greater size was desirable, we added other rooms and 'entries' on this side and on that, but gave the plan no center, no coherence. . . . But now in homes of every size the tendency is to make the hall at once beautiful and useful, the most conspicuous feature in the architectural effect and the most delightful living-room of all; not a living room like the

Williamson Cottage, Islesboro, Fred L. Savage, 1895. Photograph © 1989 by Richard Cheek for the Maine Historic Preservation Commission.

others, but one with a distinct purpose and therefore a distinct expression of its own. In our climate and with our social ways of summer-living, we absolutely require just what it can give us—a room which in its uses shall stand midway between the piazzas on the one hand and the drawings-rooms and libraries on the other; perfectly comfortable to live in when the hour means idleness, easy access from all points outside and in, largely open to breeze and view, yet with a generous hearthstone where we may find a rally-ing-point in days of cold and rain. . . . It unifies the plan while permitting it a far greater degree of variety than was possible with the old box-like scheme.[52]

At the Williamson cottage, Savage emphasized the dark, shingled overhanging second story by supporting it on pristine, white columns, a classically derived feature of the colonial revival, and by using white clapboards to sheathe the first floor. He extended the overhanging second story to create a porch below that wrapped around the end of the house to the right of the entrance. Here, as he had done at Rosserne in Northeast Harbor and would do again at the Charles Platt, Sr., cottage (1898) on Islesboro, he used oval and round colonial revival windows as accents to enliven the plane of the walls.

Early in his career (the date is uncertain), Savage arranged to have a photograph made of himself in his studio, and he prominently displayed a drawing of the Williamson cottage (see page 17). His pride in the design seems justified, for a series of commissions for cottages on Islesboro followed it.

Williamson Cottage, Islesboro, Fred L.
Savage, 1895. Photograph © 1989 by
Richard Cheek for the Maine Historic
Preservation Commission.

The Philler Cottage (1895)
and the Valle Cottage (1895–1896)

In the fall of 1895, as the caretakers were closing up the Williamson cottage after its first season, Savage and Stratton were already developing plans for two more cottages. In November 1895, the *Belfast Republican Journal* reported "Mr. Savage, the architect, has a large crew of men employed putting in the foundation at Dark Harbor" for a colonial revival cottage for George Philler, president of the First National Bank of Philadelphia.[53] The following week, the *Bangor Industrial Journal* noted "Savage & Stratton, the Mt. Desert architects and builders, are now building a $15,000 summer residence at Dark Harbor for George Filler, [sic.] of Philadelphia and are preparing plans for a house for Mr. Valle of St. Louis, to be built at the same place. Morse & Co. of this city are furnishing the finish for the Filler cottage."[54]

The Philler cottage was Savage's earliest unadulterated use of the colonial revival style. The Valle cottage, on the other hand, was a pure expression of the shingle style, and the two concurrent projects may serve to demonstrate his stylistic range. Both cottages present a broad array of the devices that make their respective styles distinct, and at first glance they seem to have little in common. A comparison, however, shows several underlying similarities. Their exteriors present contrasting sensibilities—the rigid balance and symmetry of the colonial revival versus the seemingly informal,

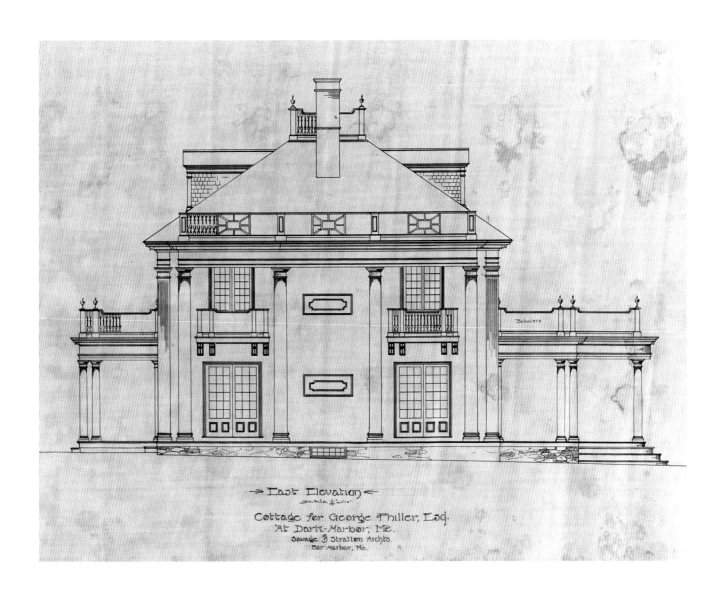

East Elevation

Cottage for George Thiller, Esq.
At Dark-Harbor, Me.
Savage & Stratton Archts.
Bar Harbor, Me.

Balusters

below and opposite: Philler Cottage,
floor plans. Courtesy of the Northeast
Harbor Library.

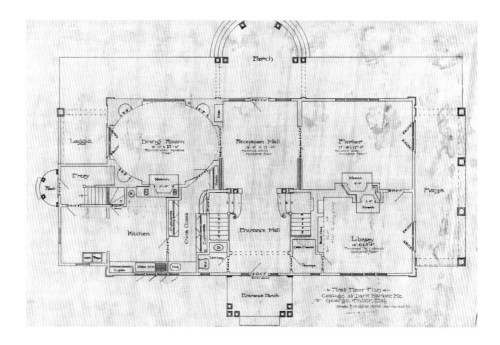

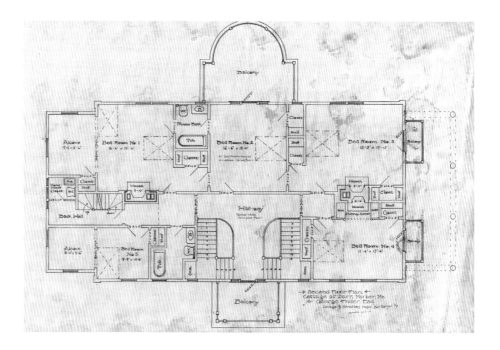

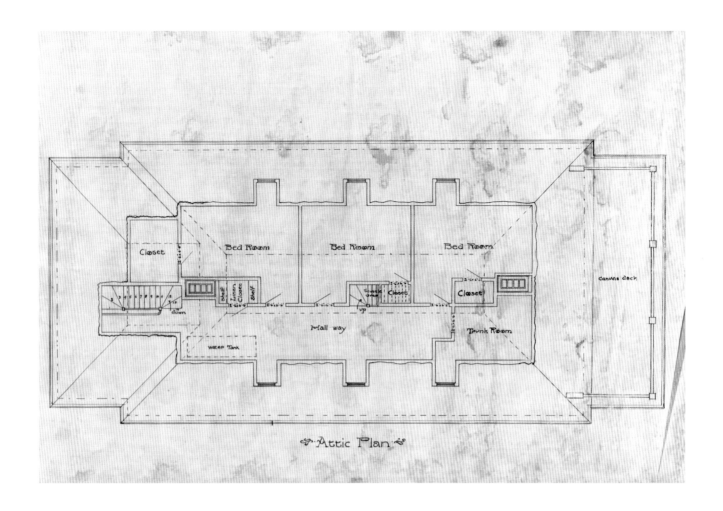

asymmetrical massing of the shingle style. But their principal rooms bear a similar relationship to one another, as do their piazzas and servants' porches and entries. Variations of the complex stairs in the entry hall of the Philler cottage would reappear at the Ledge Lawn Inn, Reverie Cove, and High Seas; the relationship of the cottage's entrance and reception hall to the library and parlor on the right and the dining room and kitchen on the left, and the piazza and water vista opposite the main entry would reappear at Breakwater and L'Escale. A round exterior feature appears in several of Savage's cottages—as the focal point of the waterside piazzas at the Williamson and Philler cottages, as a corner tower and porch at Rosserne and the Charles Platt, Sr., cottages, and as a projecting end bay on the main facade of the Valle Cottage. Savage found the round feature effective, and he used it emphatically at the George S. Silsbee Cottage, which may well be his masterpiece on Islesboro.

The Silsbee Cottage (1898–1899)

Designed for the Boston textile executive George S. Silsbee, the Silsbee Cottage is notable for a swelling stone terrace at the rear elevation—an extension of its fieldstone foundation—that visually anchors the house to the landscape and provides a podium, or base, for two projecting bays. Above this highly textured foundation, Savage used pebble-dash stucco on the exterior of the first floor; he provided another dramatic contrast by crowning the stuccoed first floor with the dark shingles and the deep shadows of a gambrel roof with flared eaves, shed dormers, and a recessed balcony tucked in between the projecting bays. Savage must have enjoyed the juxtaposition of materials, for he used a similar combination at the West Gouldsboro Library (1906, see pp. 224–225) and for his final commission, the Hauterive Garage (1921–1924, see pp. 248–259).

During the first decade of his practice, Savage had no significant, locally based competition on Islesboro or in Northeast Harbor. In both communities, he was active in the first wave of development and quickly established his reputation as a designer of seasonal cottages. But from the outset, he was drawn to Bar Harbor, and his list of clients there grew steadily. While he continued to do work in both Islesboro and Northeast Harbor at the turn of the century, the Bar Harbor summer residents soon became his main clientele. By 1898, in an article about his Islesboro and Northeast Harbor work, *the Bangor Industrial Journal* even called him "Fred L. Savage of Bar Harbor."[55]

Silsbee Cottage, Islesboro, Fred L.
Savage, 1899. Photograph © 1989 by
Richard Cheek for the Maine Historic
Preservation Commission.

Chapter III
Bar Harbor and the End of the Cottage Era (circa 1900–1924)

Savage's Later Work in the Historical Revival Styles

Bar Harbor is only nine miles from Northeast Harbor, but moving there around 1898 dramatically altered the patterns of Savage's life and work. By the late 1890s, many Bar Harbor cottages were in the hands of second or third owners; consequently, renovation and additions became an important part of his practice. His earlier work had revolved around the design or construction of new cottages, but after 1898 almost half of his commissions were for additions to existing cottages, or for different types of buildings, including stables, stores, offices, private clubs, public buildings, and garages. Stylistically his work became more diverse too, as the popularity of the shingle style was waning, and he quickly demonstrated an ability to work in various revival styles. Savage's shift toward the use of historical revival styles reflects the contemporaneous evolution of the shingle style away from its initial informality and toward a more restrained, academic expression. The "decline" or transformation of the shingle style is usually attributed to a variety of reasons, including the growing influence of schools of architecture with their emphasis on historical styles, and social and economic factors that discouraged sprawling floor plans, such as a diminished pool of live-in servants as more and more Americans entered the middle class and the imposition of the income tax.[1] Parenthetically, it is worth noting that just as he designed additions and alterations, other architects have altered buildings designed by Savage. Stone Ledge in Northeast Harbor, which Savage designed in 1892 for Miss Clara Williamson, exemplifies both this process of change and the move away from the shingle style. Savage's original cottage was altered first by Edmund Gilchrist and then in 1915 by Peabody and Stearns. The alterations, including an exuberant colonial revival tiered tower of porches, dominate the facade and metaphorically point to the passing of the shingle style.

On a personal level, Savage's move to Bar Harbor coincided with the dissolution of his first marriage. After twelve years of marriage and three children, Fred and Florence divorced, and in October 1901, he married Alice Preble, his twenty-two-year-old secretary in Bar Harbor.[2] In addition to this domestic upheaval, two catastrophic fires coincided with his relocation, so the twentieth century opened dramatically for Fred Savage.

The Kebo Valley Club (1899)

On the evening of July 1, 1899, Bar Harbor's Kebo Valley Club burned to the ground. The rambling, shingle-style clubhouse had been designed in 1888 by Wilson Eyre (1858–1944) of Philadelphia. For a decade its reading rooms, dining facilities, theater/ballroom, horse track, and golf course combined to make it a center of social activities. Less than two months after the fire, Savage had drawn plans for a new clubhouse "two stories high, of picturesque pattern, 107 x 35 feet in dimensions. The main reception room in the first story will be 28 x 35 feet with paneled ceiling. The dining rooms 16 x 27 and 13 x 13 [feet] will be up stairs. Verandas above and below will give the members and guests [a] view of the links."[3] The directors of the club selected a new site overlooking the golf course, and the original gatehouse, which had survived the fire, was moved and incorporated into the new building. (The clubhouse designed by Savage burned in 1947.)

The original Kebo Valley Clubhouse and Savage's replacement resembled the long, low, loose-jointed, and informal shingle-style clubhouses that provided a social focal point in many late nineteenth-century resorts. Today the Newport Casino (1879–1881) by McKim, Mead and White is the most famous example of the type, but Eyre and Savage would have known many others, which were frequently illustrated in the architectural press.[4]

Although Savage had private commissions in Bar Harbor prior to the Kebo Valley project, the new clubhouse brought summer people into contact with his work much as the smaller, simpler shingle-style Reading Room had done in Northeast Harbor. The general contractor, Chester Hodgkins, was still working on the clubhouse when Savage was hired to design a similar shingle-style private club just north of Bar Harbor.

Kebo Valley Club, Bar Harbor, Wilson
Eyre, 1888. Courtesy of the Bar Harbor
Historical Society.

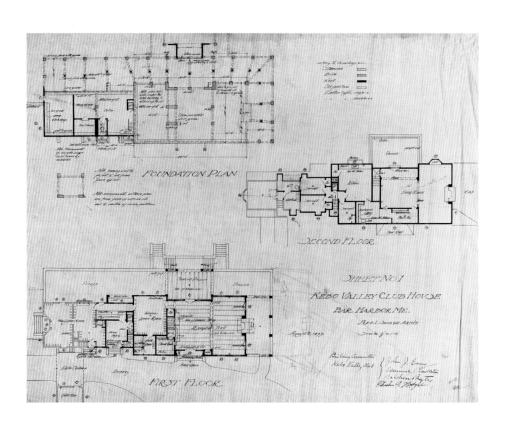

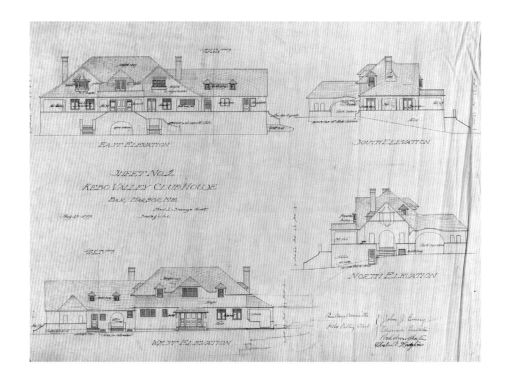

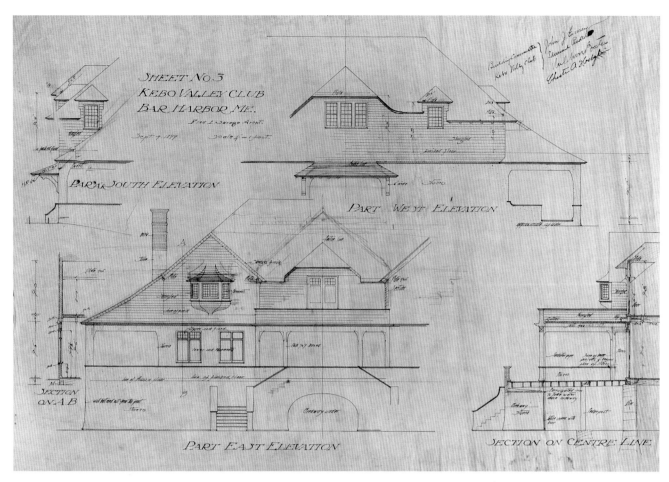

SHEET NO. 3
KEBO VALLEY CLUB
BAR HARBOR ME.

above and opposite: Kebo Valley Club, Bar Harbor, elevations and floor plans, Fred L. Savage, 1899. Courtesy of the Mount Desert Island Historical Society.

The Pot and Kettle Club (1899)

above and opposite: Pot and Kettle Club,
Bar Harbor, Fred L. Savage, 1900

In the fall of 1899, a group of businessmen from Philadelphia and New York purchased six acres of land on Hulls Cove and formed the Pot and Kettle Club. The site was far enough from town to provide a male sanctuary for eating, drinking, and convivial weekly gatherings during the months of July and August. The activities of the Pot and Kettle Club were modeled on Philadelphia's Fishhouse Club, and its facilities were simple: a kitchen, a large dining room with a fireplace, a smaller dining room, a reading and smoking lounge, and accommodations for staff under the eaves. The construction cost approximately $6,000.

Savage's design called for a building 104 feet long, 40 feet wide, framed by a covered piazza on the west facade and an open terrace on the north facade. The large dining room, which the newspaper called a living room, was

> 24 x 30 feet. . . . a spacious apartment full of windows, and on one side a large red brick fireplace five feet wide, the studding and rafters painted green and finished rough to the top. This room when finished and furnished will have a most cozy and homelike appearance. . . . In the smoking room . . . are numerous window seats, a large fireplace, on one side of which there will be a large divan. On the walls of this room there will be sheathing five feet high above which the walls will be covered with burlap. A door leads out from this room on to the piazza.[5]

Luxury was not the point. Clubs of this sort offered members a comforting sense of belonging, the pleasurable anticipation of scheduled events, and the reassurance that year after year favorite things endured—worn but comfortable furniture, familiar tableware and old paintings in quiet, sun-shafted reading rooms. From Jekyll Island, Georgia, to Maine, a constellation of such clubs provided (and continue to provide) refuges from the striving hubbub of life.[6]

Savage appears to have been a member of the Kebo Valley Club, and he was later commodore of the Bar Harbor Yacht Club.[7] Records for the Pot and Kettle Club are not available, but Savage clearly enjoyed the confidence of Edgar T. Scott, one of its four founders, who engaged Savage, while the Pot and Kettle clubhouse was still under construction, to work on his cottage in Bar Harbor.

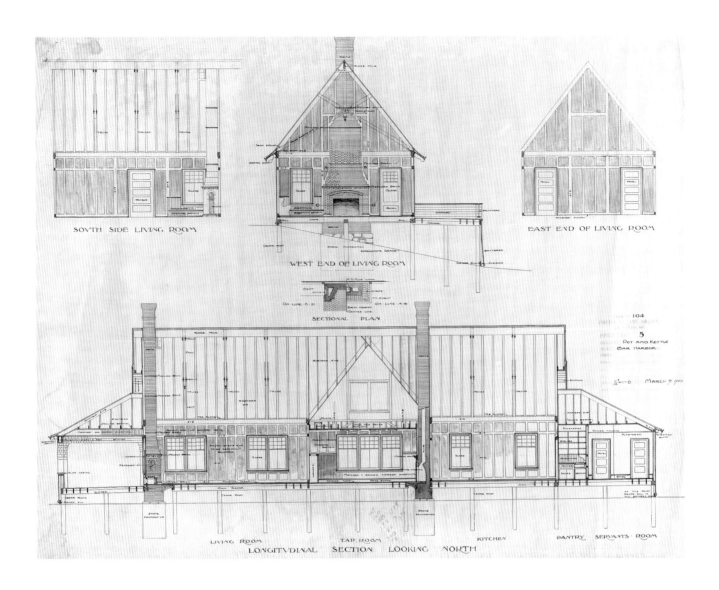

SOVTH SIDE LIVING ROOM

WEST END OF LIVING ROOM

EAST END OF LIVING ROOM

SECTIONAL PLAN

LIVING ROOM   TAP ROOM   KITCHEN   PANTRY SERVANTS ROOM

LONGITVDINAL SECTION LOOKING NORTH

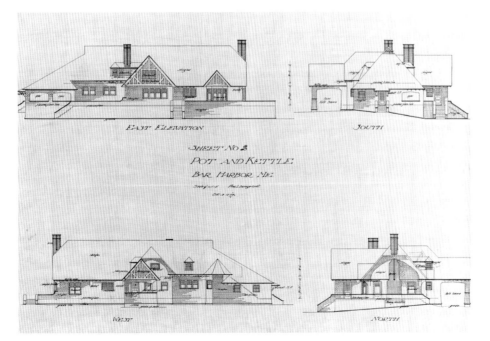

EAST ELEVATION

SOUTH

SHEET NO 2
POT AND KETTLE
BAR HARBOR ME.

WEST

NORTH

above and left: Pot and Kettle Club, elevations. Courtesy of the Mount Desert Island Historical Society.

opposite: Pot and Kettle Club

165

The Chiltern Cottage (1895)

Chiltern, the Edgar T. Scott cottage, was designed by William Longfellow (1836–1913) of Boston. Savage was the on-site, supervising architect, and he monitored the work of about thirty-five carpenters. It was not unusual for architects from Boston, Philadelphia, or New York to employ local architects to supervise the construction on site. Savage worked for many architects in this capacity, including W. R. Emerson, Rotch & Tilden, and Andrews, Jacques & Rantoul of Boston; Grosvenor Atterbury of New York; Burnam & Root of Chicago; and Furness, Evans & Company of Philadelphia. He relied on these commissions to supplement his income and must have appreciated the opportunity to gain inspiration from his contemporaries' designs.

The Chiltern project is memorable, since it involved Savage's only recorded confrontation with organized labor. About half of the men on the job were members of the Carpenters Union 459. Led by W. W. Small, E. K. Whitaker, and A. F. Townsend, they insisted that only union members be employed. When Savage's foreman, R. H. Moon, fired nine of the union men, eleven more walked off in protest.[8] Following the incident, the local newspapers published letters from the union and Savage, who refused to accept union membership as a prerequisite for employment. He said each craftsman should be able to decide whether or not he wished to join the union; furthermore, he argued that neither the employer nor the union should unduly influence that decision:

> I have made a careful study of the issues involved in many of the labor troubles in the past few years. . . . It is unjust in the employer to insist that no laborer shall belong to a union, and it is also wrong for the labor leaders to insist that no laborer shall be employed unless he belongs to a union. The labor union should be a purely voluntary organization; to make it compulsory is to violate not so much the rights of the employers, as the rights of the laborers. If the union demands that laborers be discharged because they are not union men, the demand ought to be resisted at every hazard; if the employer discharges men simply because they belong to a union, this action should be resisted by the union at all hazards. . . .
>
> The sympathy of the public should depend entirely on the demands of the union and those of the employers, and when the employer stands firm for the rights of all men alike, leaving it optional for them whether they shall join the union or not, he shall be upheld by the public because his

position is based on sound principles. But when he allows good men to be driven off his work because they do not belong to a union, he is permitting a blow to [be] struck against labor itself and will not be sustained. Had these principles been adhered to by the union men in Bar Harbor this winter, there would have been no labor trouble here.[9]

Scott and Longfellow supported Savage, and the union eventually capitulated.

During the summer of 1900 Savage was still married to Florence, living in Northeast Harbor and commuting to Bar Harbor. In addition to completing the two clubhouses and the Scott cottage, he was working on several other jobs. He was preparing additions for Mrs. John Harrison's cottage, Faraway, which had been designed in 1885 by Furness, Evans & Co. of Philadelphia; he was designing an addition for Augustus C. Gurnee to Beaudesert, a cottage that had been designed in 1881 by William R. Emerson of Boston for Gurnee's parents; and he was developing plans for two new cottages—Callendar House for J. C. Livingston (see pp. 176–181) and a cottage for George S. Robbins.[10] During the same year, Savage also worked on the new Asticou Inn in Northeast Harbor.

The Asticou Inn (1900)

above, opposite, and following spread:
Asticou Inn, Northeast Harbor,
Fred L. Savage, 1900

Fred and Florence Savage probably rented their house, Hilltop Cottage, for some or all of the 1900 season. They must have moved across the road into rooms in the Asticou Inn, for on the night of September 17, 1900, the inn burned to the ground, and the newspaper reported that "F. L. Savage and his family escaped in their night-clothes."[11] A. C. Savage decided to rebuild at once. He naturally turned to his son, and by Thanksgiving the *Bangor Industrial Journal* noted "there is a good deal of nice building going on at North East Harbor. Among the structures going up is the Asticou Inn, burned last summer and now being rebuilt, according to plans of Architect F. L. Savage."[12]

In several respects, the new Asticou Inn was a milestone in Savage's career. First, it was larger than anything he had designed or built so far. Most of his earlier cottages cost between $5,000 and $6,000. His larger, more ornate cottages such as the George Philler cottage on Islesboro might cost as much as $15,000, but the new Asticou cost $19,416.42, and A. C. Savage paid Fred a total of $2,801.01 for his work on the new inn.[13] This windfall must have helped finance Savage's permanent move to Bar Harbor. Before the inn opened for its second season, he divorced Florence, purchased a lot on Atlantic Avenue in Bar Harbor, and began construction of Vista cottage (1902) on the back of the lot. When his new cottage was ready, he married Alice Preble and built a more substantial, Tudor revival home, the Atlantean (1903, see pages 198–201), on the same lot parallel to the street and in front of Vista cottage. Just as the Tudor revival Atlantean obscured the earlier shingle-style Vista cottage, the new Asticou showed that Savage, like others of his generation, was putting the shingle style behind him at the turn of the century.

Although its walls were shingled, the exterior of the Asticou is different from Savage's earlier work. It has no classically derived ornament nor any of the curved features he had used often as points of emphasis. Instead, the exterior of the inn is symmetrical and rectilinear. Heavy brackets support the porte cochere and a low-pitched roof projects beyond the walls in a sharp, shallow plane, like the brim of a hat. The elevation is organized as a series of subtly balanced, slightly receding and projecting blocks. The composition of masses hints at his early interest in the Spanish colonial revival style that John Carrère and Thomas Hastings of New York had adapted for the Ponce de Leon (1888) and the Alcazar (1889), hotels developed by Henry M. Flagler in St. Augustine, Florida.[14] Postcards of Florida hotels survived among Savage's papers, and it is worth noting that when he enlarged Herman Savage's

Asticou Inn

Rockend Hotel in 1909, Fred Savage again used the towers, balconies, stucco, and low-pitched roofs that typified this kind of resort development in Florida.

The second Asticou is a good example of Savage's tendency to use crisp, white colonial revival interior trim no matter what style was used on the exterior. The Asticou's ground floor plan resembles the plan he often used in larger cottages, with the entry hall containing a staircase (to the right) and opening into large dining and sitting rooms. Beyond these public rooms a wall of windows and glazed French doors opened onto a broad porch overlooking the harbor. The new inn could accommodate up to sixty guests and is still in use today.

The design and construction of the Asticou Inn coincided with a burst of productivity as Savage's career gained momentum in Bar Harbor. From 1892 until 1898, he—sometimes working with Stratton—typically had one or two new cottage-related commissions each year in Bar Harbor. But during 1900 and 1901, Savage was responsible for the alterations and additions at five major Bar Harbor cottages; he also designed three new ones and emerged from this flurry as the leading architect based in Bar Harbor. Among these commissions, the most notable new cottage was the Callendar House, located near Bear Brook on Schooner Head south of Bar Harbor and designed for John Callendar Livingston. The most memorable work on an older cottage was a wing for Devilstone. These contemporaneous projects are stylistically different and demonstrate Savage's versatility as a designer.

Asticou Inn, elevation, Northeast Harbor, Fred L. Savage, 1900. Courtesy of the Northeast Harbor Library.

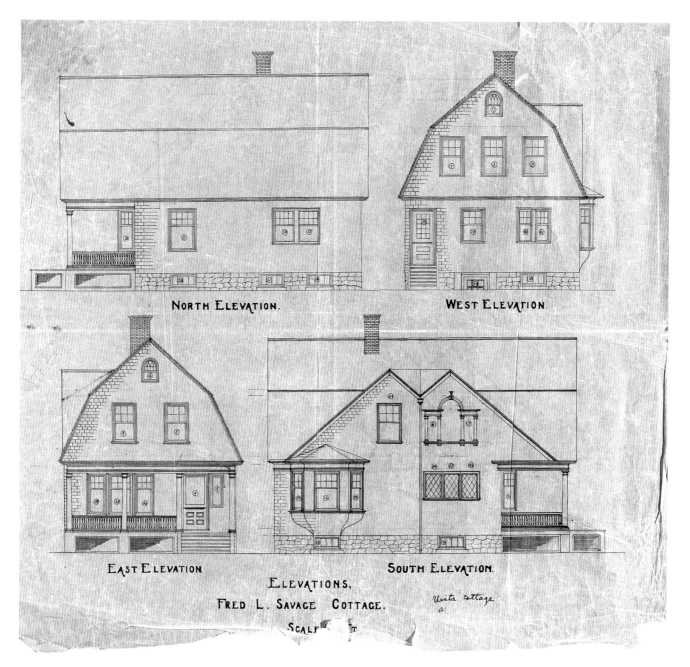

NORTH ELEVATION.

WEST ELEVATION.

EAST ELEVATION.

SOUTH ELEVATION.

ELEVATIONS,
FRED L. SAVAGE COTTAGE.
SCALE

above: Vista Cottage, Bar Harbor, elevations, Fred L. Savage, 1902. Courtesy of the Mount Desert Island Historical Society.

opposite: Vista Cottage

The Callendar House (1900–1901)

above and opposite: Callendar House, Bar Harbor, Fred. L. Savage, 1901

The *Bar Harbor Record* called the Callendar House "the most imposing" of the "six or more cottages being erected" in 1901.[15] It was the first summer cottage built of brick in Bar Harbor, and it was the most formal design Savage had produced. The brick walls, which rose from a foundation of cut granite, were laid in a carefully worked pattern of alternating headers and stretchers. The precision of the masonry was in keeping with the symmetry and balance of the elevation, which featured a gabled, projecting central bay with a Palladian window above the entrance. Crisp wooden details—the columns flanking the entry, the lintels, and window muntins—and the red slate roof all contributed to the impression of control and restraint. The reporter praised the refinement of the late colonial revival plan and ornament and called attention to modern structural features and conveniences:

> All the floors of the house are lined with fire proof deadening felt [asbestos].
> The lower sash of each window is one pane of glass. The upper sashes are
> divided into small panes. Brass pulleys with chain instead of the usual cord
> make the raising or lowering of the sashes easy, besides holding them safely in
> any position.[16]

Savage and his peers, building far from metropolitan centers of supplies, had to order up-to-date hardware, materials, and appliances, and among Savage's papers are catalogs from Detroit; Chattanooga; Saint Louis; Racine; San Diego; New York; and Winona, Minnesota.[17]

On the night of April 16, 1901, just before it was completed, the interior of the Callendar house was gutted by fire, and the following day the *Record* reported that "all that remains today of the handsome house are the four brick walls and the handsome chimneys with their fireplaces unblemished, rising straight and plumb into the air."[18] The loss was estimated to be $20,000, which would mean that it was Savage's most expensive cottage to date. Despite the fire, Livingston had Savage complete the Callendar house according to the original plans.

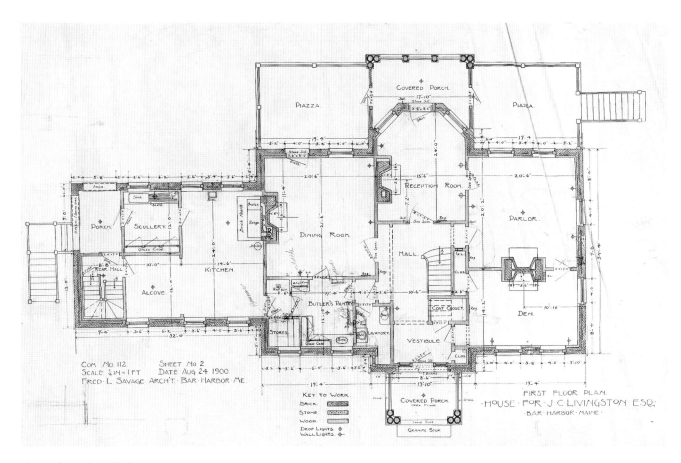

above and opposite: Callendar House,
floor plan and detail, Fred L. Savage,
1902. Courtesy of the Mount Desert
Island Historical Society.

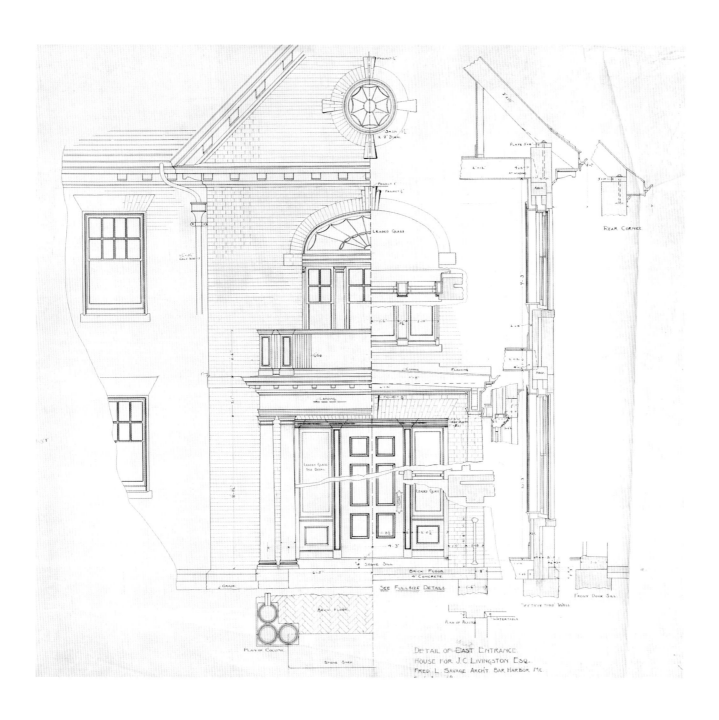

DETAIL OF EAST ENTRANCE.
HOUSE FOR J.C. LIVINGSTON ESQ.
FRED. L. SAVAGE ARCHT. BAR HARBOR ME.

REAR CORNICE

FRONT DOOR SILL

above and opposite: Catalogs from the office of Fred L. Savage. Courtesy of the Mount Desert Island Historical Society.

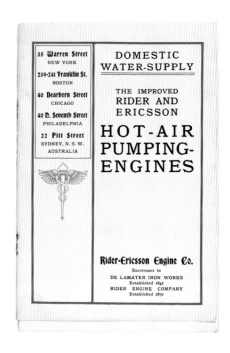

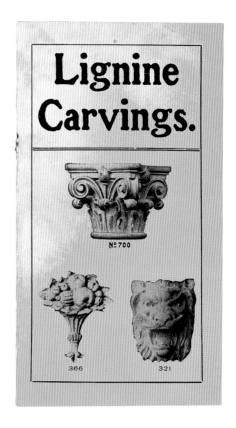

THE PHOENIX WIRE WORKS
CATALOG №35   DETROIT, MICH

The Devilstone Cottage (1901)

While the Callendar House was under construction, Savage designed additions to two cottages—Devilstone and Faraway (1886, 1901). Rotch and Tilden of Boston had designed Devilstone in 1885 for Mrs. George Bowler. It was subsequently owned by a New York banker, James T. Woodward, and then by Thomas A. Scott of Philadelphia, the fourth president of the Pennsylvania Railroad. In 1901 Savage added a wing for Scott's daughter and her husband, Clement B. Newbold. Prominently located on the shore path, Devilstone was a prestigious commission. Savage decided not to replicate the original shingle-style exterior; instead, above a stone ground floor, he used stucco and half-timbering, hallmarks of the Tudor or English revival style for the new wing, which contained a living room or library on the ground floor and bedrooms on its second floor.

The historical roots of the shingle style and the Tudor revival style are intertwined, both stemming from an interest in picturesque medieval English and seventeenth-century American colonial buildings.[19] The seeds of both styles coexist in the land elevation of Gambrill and Richardson's William Watt Sherman house (1875) in Newport where stuccoed panels are set within shingled walls; moreover, the upper floors of the Sherman house are supported by ground-floor walls made of cream-colored Roxbury pudding stone accented with dark Connecticut brownstone. For the next quarter century, designers using the shingle and the Tudor revival styles would emphasize the picturesque effect of pseudo-medieval, overhanging upper stories by using one material to sheathe the first or ground floor and a contrasting material on the walls and roof above. Beginning in the mid-1880s, the national journal *Architecture and Building* often illustrated projects with walls of shingles, half-timbered stucco, or a combination of the two above a stone-faced first floor.[20]

Several large Tudor revival cottages had been built in Bar Harbor early in Savage's career, including Chatwold (1882–1883), designed by Rotch and Tilden for Mrs. Robert P. Bowler; Tanglewold, the DeGrasse Fox cottage attributed to Emerson; and Blair Eyrie (originally called Avamaya), designed in 1895 by Sidney V. Stratton and Frank Quimby of New York. Savage had previously used half-timbering himself in gables at Brackenfell (1893) in Northeast Harbor, and he had used a stone and stuccoed base with shingles above at the Silsbee cottage (1889) on Islesboro, at Journey's End in Harborside, and at the Bird's Nest Cottage (circa 1900) at Asticou.

The emphatically Tudor revival–style Devilstone addition must have been well received; Savage used this style again the following year for his own cottage, the

Devilstone, Bar Harbor, addition by Fred
L. Savage, 1901. Courtesy of the Bar
Harbor Historical Society.

above and opposite: Devilstone, Bar
Harbor, addition by Fred L. Savage, 1901

Atlantean (1903), and for Breakwater (1903–1904), the large cottage he designed for
John I. Kane.[21] Devilstone has been largely demolished, and only the ground floor of
Savage's wing survives, a large rectangular room with windows on three elevations.
The dark woodwork—Savage called it Flemish brown—is dramatically set off against
the white walls and ceiling. The room culminates in an elaborately framed fireplace on
the west wall. On his plan, Savage referred to it as a "living room," and its design is a
more elaborate and formal version of the living rooms at Brackenfell and the Samuel A.
Eliot cottage in Northeast Harbor.

Just as the emphatic patterns of Tudor revival half-timbering are more rigid than
the flowing surfaces of the shingle style, Savage's later work in both Northeast Harbor
and Bar Harbor is often more formal than his earlier cottages, reflecting his sensitive
response to nuances of time and place. Two late shingle-style commissions, Sunni
Holme and Grey Rock, illustrate his growing tendency to define forms sharply—to
use linear shadows and ornament to create a precise sense of volume and plane.

Devilstone, Bar Harbor, addition by Fred
L. Savage, detail, elevations, and floor
plan. Courtesy of the Bar Harbor
Historical Society.

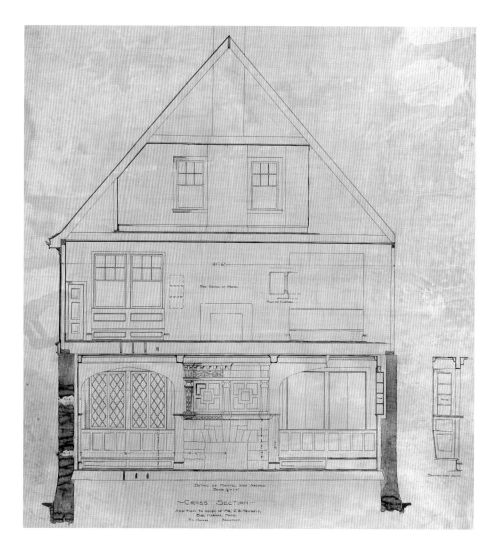

ALTERATIONS TO HOUSE
MR. C.B.NEWBOLD.
BAR HARBOR, MAINE.
F.L. SAVAGE, ARCHITECT.
COMMISSION No. 132.

WEST ELEVATION.
Scale ¼"=1'0'.

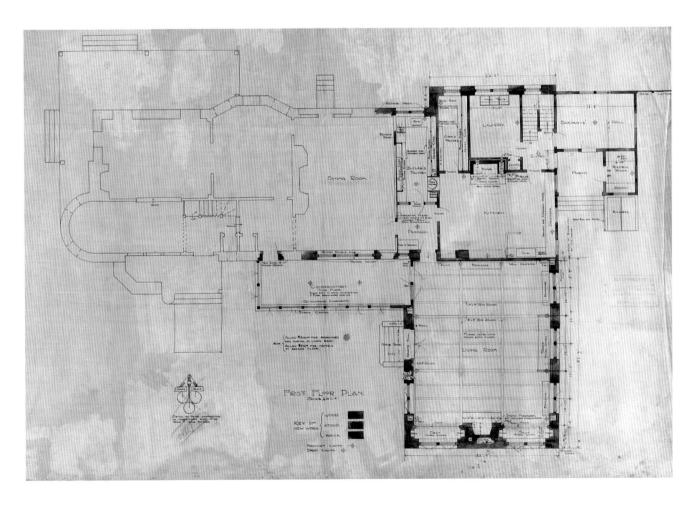

DINING ROOM.

LAUNDRY.

KITCHEN.

LIVING ROOM.

FIRST FLOOR PLAN.
Scale ¼"=1'0".

"Chatwold," Bar Harbor, Me

Chatwold, Bar Harbor, Rotch & Tilden,
1883. Courtesy of the Bar Harbor
Historical Society.

Blair Fyrie, Bar Harbor, Stratton and
Quimby, 1895. Courtesy of the Bar Harbor
Historical Society.

above: Tanglewold, Bar Harbor, DeGrasse
Fox, 1888. Courtesy of the Bar Harbor
Historical Society.

opposite: Bird's Nest, Northeast Harbor,
Fred L. Savage, 1900

Sunni Holme (1901) and Grey Rock (1911)

above and opposite: Sunnie Holme, also known as the James H. Falt Cottage, Northeast Harbor, Fred L. Savage, 1901

Sunni Holme (as Savage spelled the cottage name on his drawings) was designed in 1901 for James H. Falt, a manager of the Rockend Hotel, in Northeast Harbor. It is asymmetrical in plan and elevation and has interesting shingle-style details; nonetheless, it has close neighbors, is compact, and in general more formal than most of the earlier Harborside houses.

The exterior is shingled with a flared overhang defining the second story. As at Brackenfell and Journey's End, Sunni Holme has two projecting bays of different form and finish—in this case a larger gabled bay to the left with a porch below and a projecting bay window above. To the right of the central entry is a three-sided, two-story bay capped by a peaked roof. The central entry, flanked by sidelights, is a classic Savage Dutch door. As he did so often, Savage designed the windows here with small panes in the upper sash and a single pane in the lower sash. Sunni Holme's memorable details include decoratively sawn curved brackets beneath the eaves and a curved and shingled bracket supporting the overhanging second story on the western facade.

Grey Rock, designed for William S. Grant in Northeast Harbor in 1911, is one of Savage's cottages on the shore. Its two elongated wings form a shallow V, and although it has a traditional shingle-style stone foundation, the upper floors are memorable for the visually precise division of each element of the elevation. Here Savage used asbestos—then a new material—panels and shingles on an exterior that is reminiscent of his work at Devilstone.

The increasing balance and repose in Savage's work may reflect his use of geometry as well as the popularity of historical revival styles. A preliminary sketch for additions to Grasslands shows he was using equilateral triangles to organize the facade. The Grasslands drawing (circa 1905) is undated, rough, and unsigned; nonetheless, it suggests that Savage was aware of the early-twentieth-century theories of Dynamic Symmetry—an idea promoted by Jay Hambidge (1867–1924) stating that the key to the art of classical Greece lay in Euclidian geometry using the diagonals of squares and rectangles—and the growing interest in the use of geometry in the graphic arts and architecture.[22]

In keeping with the increasing formality of his work after moving to Bar Harbor, Savage began to use precisely cut granite instead of the irregular beach cobbles and surface boulders that so effectively had expressed the organic quality of the shingle style. He had an economic as well as a stylistic interest in finely worked granite: according to the letterhead of a sheet of business stationery he served as the manager of the Bear Brook granite quarry.[23]

BAR HARBOR, ME., *Oct. 19th* 1900

BEAR BROOK QUARRY,

FRED L. SAVAGE, MANAGER.

RICH BROWN SEAM FACE & BLUE GRAY GRANITE.

SOLD TO *Mr. A. E. Lawrence.*

May 26 To 30 ft. of Curbing, @ 35¢ per ft.	$10	50

Invoice, Bear Brook Quarry, Fred L.
Savage, Manager, October 19, 1900.
Courtesy of Raymond Strout.

Grey Rock, also known as the William
S. Grant Cottage, Northeast Harbor,
Fred L. Savage, 1911

The Faraway Cottage (1900)

At the same time the Callendar House and the addition at Devilstone were under way, Savage was also working as design architect and general contractor for a major addition at Faraway, the H. C. Hart cottage on Eagle Lake Road in Bar Harbor. This shingle-style cottage had been designed in 1886 by Furness, Evans & Company of Philadelphia. In 1900, working for a new owner, Mrs. John Harrison, Savage added a seventy-by-twenty-eight-foot wing "virtually transforming the present structure into one of the larger residences of the village."[24] On the exterior he used clapboards on the first story and shingles above in keeping with the original house, but it was the quality of the interior colonial revival details that drew attention and praise from the local press:

> In size the dining room is 17 by 28 feet. In finish the details are purely colonial and are very elaborate. Fluted ionic columns topped with carved capitals and elliptic arches, adorn the walls. A handsome wainscoting extends around the room, the walls of which are finished in panels. On one side of the room is a large open fire-place and a mantel designed in strict details of the other finish. An elaborate frieze of scroll work extends the full width of the mantel. Surmounting the shelf is a plate glass mirror set in a carved gilt frame.[25]

Catalogues among his papers suggest that Savage sometimes ordered stock millwork, but sketches and full-size shop patterns among his drawings show that he also designed custom ornament. He often used colonial revival interior ornament for shingle-style houses as he did here—Journey's End and L'Escale are other good examples—and this contrasting treatment of the exterior and interior on the same house was endorsed by his clientele.

Woodland grove, Acadia National Park

The Atlantean Cottage (1903)

Savage's home, the Tudor revival–style Atlantean, was designed shortly after the new Asticou Inn opened, and it presented him as a revival-style architect to potential clients in Bar Harbor. The *Bar Harbor Record* called it "An Old English Design Worked out Most Effectively" and published a detailed description that Savage must have provided.[26] The cottage's foundations and first floor are faced with finely cut granite, while the second-story gables and dormers are sheathed with stucco and Tudor revival half-timbering. The facade is balanced and formal. In Savage's plan the central entry opens into a spacious reception hall (seventeen by eighteen feet) with a staircase across the wall opposite the entrance. This hall provides access to a bathroom beneath the stair landing, a dining room (sixteen by eighteen feet) on the left, and a parlor (sixteen by twenty feet) on the right. A den or study, a butler's pantry, kitchen, servants' dining room, and porch occupy the rear of the first floor. On the second floor is another bathroom and the four principal bedrooms, each with one or more closets and an open fireplace. The third floor contains five servants' bedrooms, a bathroom, trunk room, and storage for linens. The basement was fitted with sinks and drains for a laundry as well as another servants' bathroom.

Savage published the Atlantean in the nationally circulated *Scientific American Building Monthly*. According to the description accompanying his plans and photographs, the Bear Mountain granite of the first story was set in red mortar, the exterior half-timbering was finished with "hard oil and stain," and the shingles on the roof were stained "a dull shade of moss green." This article also describes the woodwork in the entrance hall as oak "treated in a Flemish brown" with a "plate rack extending around the hall at the height of five feet, from which perpendicular strips descend at various intervals to the base, forming wall spaces which are covered with crimson burlap . . . the wall space above is tinted to harmonize."[27]

Savage sited the Atlantean on the street to show potential clients what he could do, and just as Hilltop, his first home in Northeast Harbor, was followed by commissions for larger shingle-style cottages, the Atlantean was followed by the Breakwater cottage.

THE HALL.

RESIDENCE OF FREDERICK L. SAVAGE, ESQ., BAR HARBOR, ME.—See page 60.

MR. FREDERICK L. SAVAGE, ARCHITECT.

above and opposite: Atlantean. *Scientific American Building Monthly* (March, 1904), 56. Courtesy of the Northeast Harbor Library.

The Breakwater Cottage (1903–1904)

above and opposite: Breakwater, Bar Harbor, Fred L. Savage, 1904

Designed for John Innes Kane, the great-grandson of the fur tycoon John Jacob Astor, Breakwater was the largest cottage Savage designed in Bar Harbor, with a plan totaling about 13,500 square feet. Breakwater and the Devilstone wing mark the beginning of a decade in which he worked for a series of very wealthy clients. He continued to seek and accept all types of work, but for the most wealthy clients he typically designed service buildings, altered existing cottages, or served as superintending architect directing the construction of designs prepared by others. In that sense, Breakwater is atypical, for here Savage designed everything. Its massing, especially on the east elevation, and the Tudor revival treatment of the exterior walls expand and refine ideas he had introduced at the Atlantean.

No written documents survive concerning the construction of Breakwater, but the drawings and the work itself indicate the ease with which Savage made the transition to a larger, more opulent scale. The budget allowed him to include carved verge boards, leaded glass windows and doors, an extensive cut-stone base of granite with smooth, or fine-hammered, details set against the texture of rough-hammered walls. The main floor has features we expect in large cottages by Savage, including a smoking room, den, or study, adjacent the main entry, and a foyer that leads into a living hall with fireplace, beamed ceiling, a complex staircase, and access to the dining room, parlor, and seaside piazza. The long and narrow butler's pantry, tucked in between the dining room and kitchen, is fitted with cabinets and counters made of varnished Southern yellow pine. The second floor contains five bedrooms, five bathrooms, a sitting room, a laundry room, and a large balcony. Six smaller bedrooms, five bathrooms, and a sitting room occupy the third floor. In addition to the cottage, Savage designed a stable with living quarters above and a barn for the four-acre estate.

Breakwater is the best surviving example of Savage's work for wealthy clients. The two cottages he built for George Washington Vanderbilt on the grounds of Pointe d'Acadie—the J. B. Trevor cottage, Whileaway (1901–1902), and the William Jay Schieffelin cottage, Islescote (1902)—have been demolished. These Vanderbilt cottages were designed by A. W. Longfellow of Boston, and Savage was in "general charge of all the work, providing material and employing" more than a hundred men to build the cottages and implement a plan for the grounds by the Olmsted firm.[28]

This work at Pointe d'Acadie was Savage's largest job as a general contractor. (Longfellow, the design architect, had F. A. Lovejoy on site as a supervising architect.) Smaller projects for wealthy clients include the carriage house (1902–1903) he

above and opposite: Breakwater

designed for Four Acres, the estate of A. J. Cassatt, president of the Pennsylvania railroad (and brother of the painter Mary Cassatt), and Buonriposo (1904), a cottage originally designed by Grosvenor Atterbury of New York for Ernesto G. Fabbri, husband of Edith Shepard, who was George Vanderbilt's niece. Buonriposo burned in 1918, and Savage directed the construction of its replacement in 1919, using a design provided by the owner. (The second Buonriposo was demolished in 1963.) Savage also directed the construction of a cottage for Anne Archbold, daughter of John D. Archbold, president of the Standard Oil Company (1896–1911).

Breakwater

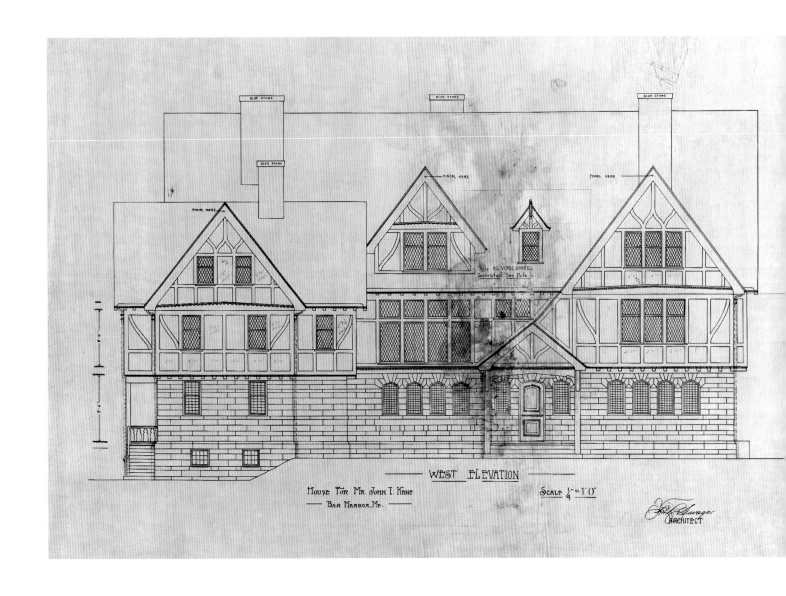

WEST ELEVATION

HOUSE FOR MR. JOHN I. KANE
— BAR HARBOR, ME. —

SCALE ¼" = 1' 0"

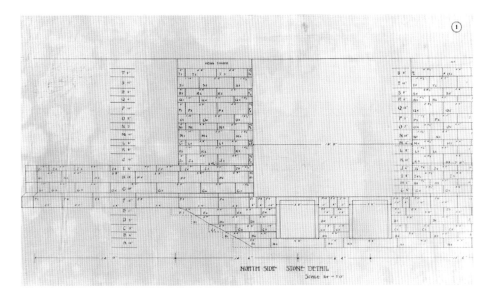

NORTH SIDE STONE DETAIL

Breakwater, elevation and stone detail.
Courtesy of the Mount Desert Island
Historical Society.

above and opposite: Breakwater

The Archbold Cottage (1903–1904)

The Archbold cottage was destroyed in the great fire of October 21, 1947 (see page 262), but surviving drawings and photographs suggest it was Savage's most exotic, unusual commission. Anne Archbold was educated abroad and developed a sincere interest in the arts. In addition to her interest in European art, she traveled to Tibet, went to Hong Kong, and commissioned a replica of a fifteenth-century Chinese junk. She also mounted expeditions to the Spice Islands, the Moluccas, and Melanesia gathering flora and fauna.[29] As the *Bar Harbor Record* reported, "the idea for her cottage was conceived from the beautiful castles in Italy, and in Paris a tiny model, perfect in every detail, was made of the proposed villa."[30] This model presumably guided Savage as he prepared the drawings, and he must have described the design to the reporter. The basement of the villa-like building contained the kitchen, pantry, closets, and servants' quarters, while the living room and a suite of bedrooms were on the principal floor. The second floor was especially striking, for from the owner's bedroom,

a spiral iron staircase leads to the tower above, where a beautiful panorama of mountain, forest and ocean spreads out before the eye. Opening from this room is a large bath room with tiled tub set deep, after the old Roman fashion and reached by several steps....

The center of the second floor is occupied by the loggia, which will be a delightful place when completed. The floor is to be tiled and the sides of glass, which will open readily so that a cool breeze can sweep across. Opening from the loggia is a long, narrow balcony which later will be hung with trailing vines and blossoms. At the back a cement stairway leads from the loggia to the terrace below. This terrace will be one of the most interesting features of the house. It fills the "hollow" of the square. A narrow, open walk the height of the second story rooms surrounds it and is upheld by twelve arches of stucco work, ornamented with carved wheels and surmounted with handsome panels of carved wood. [At] [t]he center of the terrace a fountain will play and the entire enclosure will be covered with grass. Beyond the terrace a large plot will be devoted to the garden which will be in keeping with the other appointments.[31]

The newspaper noted that the Archbold cottage was "one of the most unique houses ever built in the village, and one that is perhaps, for its size, the most

Archbold Cottage, Bar Harbor,
Fred L. Savage supervising architect,
1904. Courtesy of the Bar Harbor
Historical Society.

expensive." The plan may have been influenced by the Venetian palace–like home and museum designed by Willard T. Sears in 1899 for the art collector Isabella Stewart Gardner in Boston. Even if that is true, the Mount Desert cottage also reflected Anne Archbold's interests that ranged far beyond Boston or New England. Like Breakwater, the Archbold cottage suggests that the shingle style was too parochial for Savage's wealthiest clients in Bar Harbor.

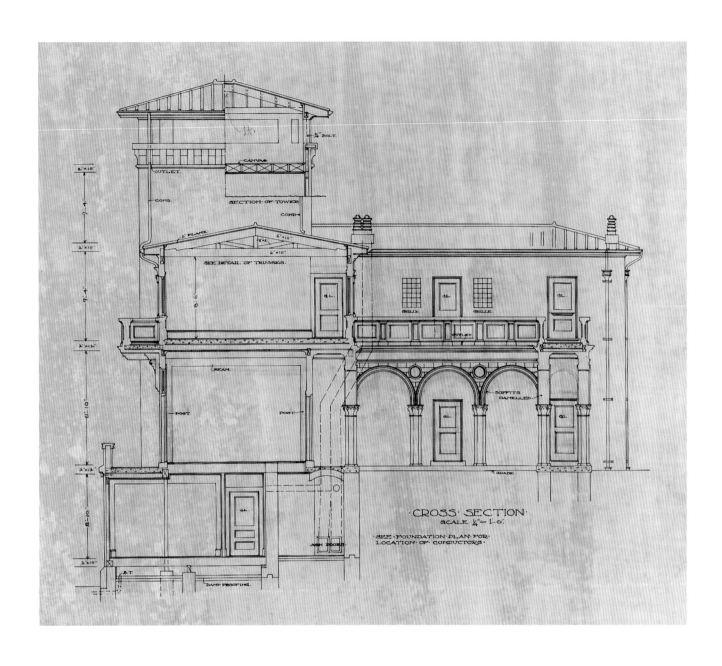

CROSS·SECTION·
SCALE ¼"= 1'-0'.
·SEE·FOUNDATION·PLAN·FOR·
LOCATION·OF·CONDUCTORS·

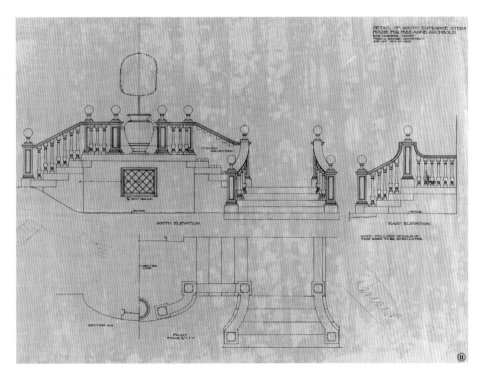

Archbold Cottage, detail and cross section, 1904. Courtesy of the Mount Desert Island Historical Society.

above and opposite: Archbold Cottage.
Courtesy of the Bar Harbor Historical
Society.

The Preservation Movement
on Mount Desert

The steady flow of work during the period of 1900 to 1914, and the financially profitable commissions from wealthy clients meant that Savage and his new wife could afford to live well during the first decade of the twentieth century, as records of Savage's vacations suggest. On October 26, 1904, the *Bar Harbor Record* reported that he and his wife would winter in California. The following fall he bought a camp in Greenville, Maine, an area famous for hunting and fishing. And the next spring (1906) he was fishing on Moosehead Lake. By 1911 Fred's older brother Herman, owner of the Rockend Hotel in Northeast Harbor, also owned the Alba Court Inn in New Symrna, Florida. The Fred Savages spent at least two months there in 1913, and they wintered in Florida again in 1917.[32] These scattered records suggest prosperity, and the years between 1904 and 1914 were probably the financial peak of Savage's career. Even then, however, he must have sensed that things were changing. The first decade of the twentieth century was marked by a serious decline in cottage construction, shifting the focus of Savage's architectural work to other building types. During the same time, it was also becoming apparent that growing efforts to preserve the landscape would, if successful, limit architectural work on Mount Desert.

President Charles W. Eliot offered the earliest thoughtful analysis of what he viewed as the adverse impact of modern technologies on Mount Desert. He was saddened when he returned to the island in 1903 to find trees cut, poles erected, and wires strung along his favorite drives. He wrote an essay that fall, which he had privately printed and distributed to island residents.[33] In this pamphlet, he identified forces that would transform Savage's career and influence development on Mount Desert for the next century.

Eliot argued that residents should be prompted by their own economic self-interest to consider the aesthetic and recreational interests of summer people when making decisions that affected the landscape. He pointed out types of employment that depended on a healthy tourist industry—architecture and construction among them—and observed that transient, short-term visitors and those who stayed longer contributed in different ways to the economy, but that all tourists were drawn by the beauty of the setting and the chance to experience nature on the water, along the shore, in the woods, or on the mountains. Since the prosperity of the region was tied to tourism, and tourism depended on identifiable aspects of the natural and built environments, he argued for conservation as an object of public policy. He urged, for example, that public access to the shore be maintained, that a system of hiking trails and scenic loop roads be built, and that bridges and roadsides be designed for beauty as well as function. He observed that wires and poles and the new automobiles—anything reminiscent of city life—detracted from the very reasons tourists sought Mount Desert.

Before writing this pamphlet in 1904, President Eliot had already started to act on his beliefs. In 1901, acting as a representative of the Northeast Harbor Village Improvement Society, he instigated the formation of the Hancock County Trustees of Public Reservations, a non-profit land conservation trust that was chartered by the state of Maine in 1903. Representatives of the Seal Harbor and Bar Harbor societies joined the Northeast Harbor Village Improvement Society in the new organization. All of the ten people that attended the first meeting were seasonal residents, and half of them were, or soon would be, Savage's clients. Savage himself, however, like other year-round residents, watched the development of the conservation movement from the outside.

Eliot was elected president of the new organization, and George B. Dorr became its vice president and executive officer. The Hancock County Trustees of Public Reservations set itself the goal to preserve the natural setting that had drawn artists and then rusticators to Mount Desert, and the trustees started to assemble parcels of scenic land on Mount Desert. Eventually these were deeded to the nation in 1916, and Acadia National Park is the fruition of their vision.[34] The first pieces of land that the trustees received were two small parcels—a square rod atop a cliff on Cooksey Drive and a hilltop overlooking Jordan Pond. The Bowl (a mountain lake) and the adjacent Beehive (a headland overlooking Sand Beach) were deeded to the trustees as a gift by Mrs. Charles Homans of Boston in 1908. The same year the trustees were also able to purchase an eighty-five-acre tract encompassing the summit of Cadillac Mountain (then called Green Mountain) because "a great speculative enterprise involving it [had] recently come to an end."[35]

The movement did not proceed without obstacles, however. In 1913 Dorr was warned that developers, believing conservation threatened their livelihoods, had "introduced a bill in the state legislature . . . to annul the charter of our Trustees of Public Reservations corporation." He rushed to Augusta, the state capital, and was able to defeat the bill; nonetheless, it was a close call, and it alarmed the trustees. They realized they could not depend on the state to perpetuate the trust, so they decided to deed their land to the federal government. Dorr later wrote, "it is here that the story of our National Park begins, born of the attack upon our Public Reservations' charter."[36]

Aside from his dedication to the Hancock County Trustees of Public Reservations, Eliot also worked with prominent members of the summer community to ban automobiles from the island, an effort that was controversial but largely successful from 1903 until 1915, when the state legislature settled the matter by forbidding towns to exclude motorists. Voters in the Town of Bar Harbor broke the ban and permitted automobiles to use their roads in 1913, but the Town of Mount Desert, comprised of the villages of Northeast Harbor and Somesville, enforced their anti-automobile ordinance until it was nullified by the state. Bar Harbor reporters kept score of the traffic during the summer of 1914:

> On Sunday between the hours of 1 and 5 PM, 151 automobiles, 22 two-horse vehicles, 81 one-horse vehicles and four motor cycles passed the plain clothes officer who was stationed on the Bay drive at the bluffs. Twenty-one automobiles came along a little later in one lot . . . there was on Monday 91 non-resident automobiles in town that will remain for the season. . . . There are 112 automobiles owned by residents for public and private use."

Several weeks later as the peak season approached: "Two hundred sixty-nine automobiles, 35 two horse teams, 86 single hitches and 15 motor cycles passed the Bluffs on Eden street Sunday afternoon between the hours of 1 and 5." And, "During the month of August 499 automobiles arrived in Bar Harbor not including those owned or used here."[37]

People in favor of cars argued that more traffic meant more business. Savage, however, would have been keenly aware that there was no correlation between automobile traffic and architectural commissions. In fact, the automobile controversy coincided with the end of the cottage boom that had sustained his career. During his practice, 110 newsworthy cottages were built or renovated in Bar Harbor. As designer or as superintending architect, Savage was responsible for twenty-five of these projects, and working in partnership with Stratton, he participated in three more jobs. His nearest competitor was the Boston firm of Andrews, Jacques (later Andrews, Jacques & Rantoul) who designed twenty-three Bar Harbor cottages during Savage's career. According to notices in the newspapers, 40 of these 110 cottages were built during the 1890s, and work intensified just as Savage established himself in Bar Harbor, with thirty-six cottages being built or renovated during the years from 1900 to 1905. After

Stanley Brooke Bridge,
Acadia National Park

1905 construction slowed dramatically: there were only six jobs related to large cottages during the period from 1906 to 1910, only five jobs during the period from 1911 to 1915, only two jobs during the period from 1916 to 1920, and only one significant job between 1921 and 1925.[38]

This dramatic decline in construction suggests that wealthy summer people were losing interest in Bar Harbor as early as 1905, but nobody can cite a specific cause for the end of the cottage era. Perhaps the cumulative, sobering effects of the Progressive movement led by Theodore Roosevelt prompted cottagers and potential cottagers to reassess their priorities; the financial panic of 1907 also must have been a factor. In any event, on Mount Desert cottage construction began to decline a full decade prior to World War I. Savage would design one of the last major cottages, High Seas, in 1911, but by then he had already shifted focus: public buildings would provide his major commissions during the final phase of his career.

Savage's Public Buildings

Savage designed most of the major public buildings on Mount Desert during the first two decades of the twentieth century, and this series of commissions shows his reputation among local officials. Savage had established himself by producing informal, shingle-style plans for seasonal visitors who wanted to get away from city life, but his final significant designs consisted of a series of formal, brick, institutional plans for local residents seeking the benefits of urban life. Like the pin of a hinge, his later work represents a turning point as the new century brought with it the changes noted by Eliot.

Bar Harbor High School,
Fred L. Savage, 1906

The West Gouldsboro Library (1906)

below: West Gouldsboro Library, Fred L. Savage, elevations and plan, 1906. Courtesy of the Northeast Harbor Library.

In 1906 Savage was commissioned to design a small library for West Gouldsboro, a little community just east of Mount Desert. He designed an intimately scaled Tudor revival building with a stone base, stuccoed walls, and a half-timbered gable over the entry. The library's facade is dominated by tactile details such as a curved hood and carved brackets above the entry and a flared cobblestone foundation reminiscent of the Union Church in Northeast Harbor. Too small to appear as formal as Breakwater, or to a lesser extent, the Atlantean, the West Gouldsboro Library is gemlike and appealing.[39] Although it is small, the West Gouldsboro library is significant as an early example of the public buildings that became a major feature of the final phase of Savage's career.

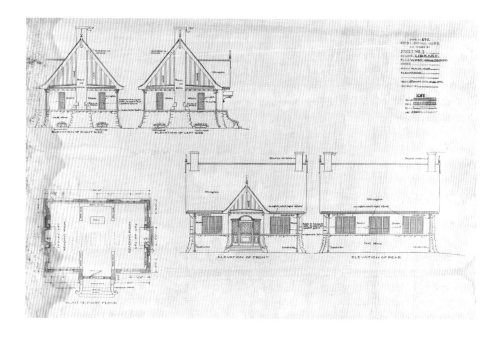

West Gouldsboro Library

The Bar Harbor High School (1907)

The largest of Savage's public buildings was the Bar Harbor High School, which replaced an existing school that was crowded and had neither a ventilation system nor any rooms equipped to teach science. The project was approved by the voters at the 1906 town meeting, and Savage was hired as its architect. He prepared a three-story floor plan that was bid using three different structural systems. The estimated cost to erect the building on a concrete foundation with brick exterior and brick interior partition walls; steel joists; and cast, reinforced concrete trim was $62,000. The two other options—using a timber frame above the concrete foundation with a clapboard exterior, or building with a wooden frame and interior partitions and stuccoed exterior walls—cost less, but town officials chose to use the fire-resistant brick and steel version.

The High School, which houses town offices today, is 82 by 120 feet and was intended to accommodate 215 to 220 students. Savage had never designed a school before and must have consulted books on the subject. The school clearly reflects German ideas promoted by Edward Robert Robson (1835–1917), an English architect whose writings were influential in creating brick, urban, turn-of-the-century schools as a recognizable building type. As principal architect for the London School Board (1871–1889) and subsequently as a consultant for the English National Education Department, Robson traveled extensively in Europe, America, and the British Isles gathering data on primary and secondary educational buildings. His book, *School Architecture* (1874), had a profound influence on school design in both England and America from around 1875 to 1930.[40]

Robson promoted designs that promised to implement ideals of universal education embodied in the English Elementary Education Act of 1870. The schools created under the act became such a prominent feature of English cityscapes that Conan Doyle had Sherlock Holmes describe the "big, isolated clumps of buildings rising above the slates, like brick islands in a lead-colored sea . . . out of which will spring the wiser, better England of the future."[41] Robson wrote about the challenge of designing schools for the urban poor, discussing the costs of construction and operation and analyzing how design affects health and behavior and how plans can help or hinder different instructional techniques. He reviewed designs in America, Scotland, Ireland, France, Germany, Austria, and England, and unequivocally endorsed schools in Saxony and Prussia as "on the whole, the best."[42]

Characteristics of German schools that he singled out for praise included the extensive use of brick, lighting, ventilation, small classrooms and large

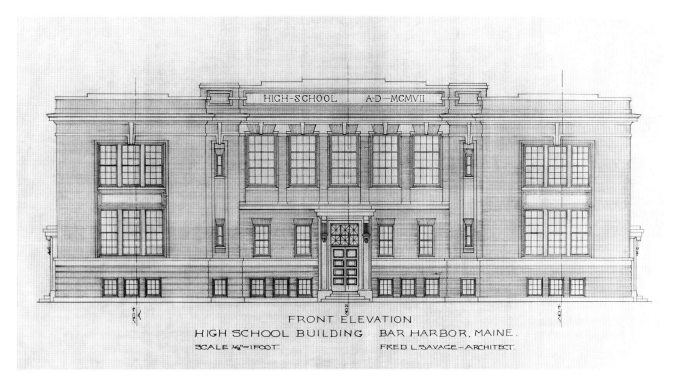

FRONT ELEVATION
HIGH SCHOOL BUILDING   BAR HARBOR, MAINE.
SCALE ⅛"=1FOOT.   FRED L. SAVAGE–ARCHITECT.

227

assembly halls, and buildings three stories high. Citing a German study of myopia, Robson said

> that a class-room is only well lighted when it has 30 square inches of glass
> to every square foot of floor-space. Taken in conjunction with other consider-
> ations, this would shew that each scholar should have the advantage of about
> 300 square inches of window glass. The calculation is very rough, and
> cannot be accepted as a rule, for much depends on the position of the glass.
> It serves, however, to shew the kind of attention now paid to this branch of
> school planning.[43]

As a result, banks of windows like those in the Bar Harbor High School are typical in designs influenced by Robson and his followers.

Concerning the importance of ventilation, Robson cites "Dr. Theodore Beckar, in the programme of the gymnasium at Darmstadt" stating that

> each boy emits, in the process of breathing, two-thirds of a cubic foot…
> of carbonic acid gas every hour. Thus, in one of our single class-rooms, con-
> taining 40 children, poisonous gas would be produced at the rate of nearly 27
> cubic feet per hour… respiration of the same air a second time is always
> unpleasant. … Even when occurring in less degree, as in rooms where partial
> ventilation exists, much of the restlessness, inattention and apparent stupidi-
> ty, often observable among the children, is due more to want of freshness in
> the air than to dullness in the scholar.[44]

Robson's influence is evident in the special attention given to ventilation: in the base-ment two so-called "Fresh Air" rooms receive fresh air from outside which is then distributed throughout the building by vertical flues or chases.

Designing the exterior elevations, Savage used brick and concrete to suggest classical forms. The rusticated raised basement, pilasters, entablature, and parapet all allude to old, revered ornamental forms that were used frequently in colonial and Federal American buildings. Horizontally the elevations are bilaterally symmetrical, and they are divided vertically into the classical tripartite pattern of base, body or shaft, and capital. These balanced facades evoke a sense of *gravitas,*

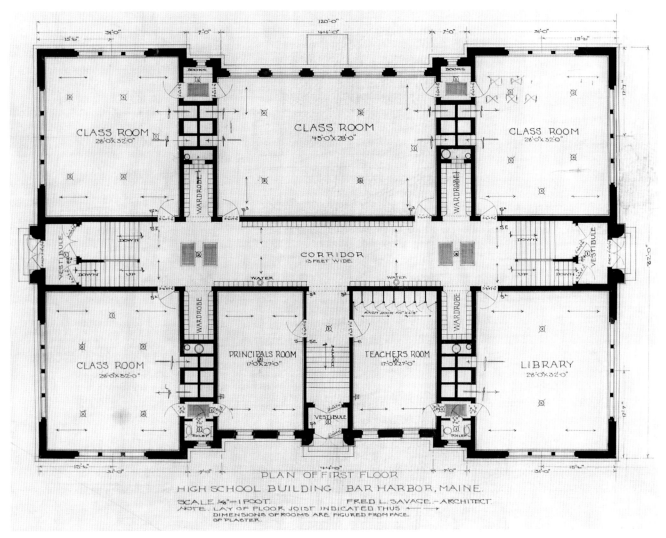

CLASS ROOM
28'-0"X32'-0"

CLASS ROOM
45'-0"X28'-0"

CLASS ROOM
28'-0"X32'-0"

WARDROBE

WARDROBE

VESTIBULE

DOWN

DOWN

UP

SE

CORRIDOR
13 FEET WIDE

SE

DOWN

UP

DOWN

VESTIBULE

WATER

WATER

WARDROBE

WARDROBE

CLASS ROOM
28'-0"X32'-0"

PRINCIPALS ROOM
17'-0"X27'-0"

TEACHERS ROOM
17'-0"X27'-0"

LIBRARY
28'-0"X32'-0"

VESTIBULE

TOILET

TOILET

PLAN OF FIRST FLOOR
HIGH SCHOOL BUILDING BAR HARBOR, MAINE.
SCALE 1/8"=1 FOOT.   FRED L. SAVAGE.—ARCHITECT.
NOTE. LAY OF FLOOR JOIST INDICATED THUS ——→
DIMENSIONS OF ROOMS ARE FIGURED FROM FACE
OF PLASTER.

Bar Harbor High School, floor plan, 1906.
Courtesy of the Mount Desert Island
Historical Society.

and their durable materials express the community's commitment to public
education.

The high school was well received, and Savage was called back, as it were, to
perform architectural encores with the Washington Normal School (1910) in Machias,
the brick Fire Department building (1911) in Bar Harbor, and the Stetson Grammar
School (1915) in Northeast Harbor.[45]

The Bar Harbor Fire Department Building <small>(1911)</small>

The Bar Harbor Fire Department building is conceptually practical and physically substantial. Like the Callendar House, it is built of brick laid in an alternating pattern of headers and stretchers. The principal facade consists of four large arched openings for the fire engines and the base of a tower that was used to hang and dry the hoses. (The upper portion of the tower was removed in the 1950s.) The windows of the firemen's quarters, which occupy the second floor, are balanced above the fire engine doors. In addition to the precision of the brickwork, notable details include the granite belt course and curved brackets between the first and second stories, the granite coping at the parapet, and the large and complexly cut granite bollards that flank the fire engine doors.

Fire Engine House, Bar Harbor, Fred L. Savage, 1911. Courtesy of the Bar Harbor Historical Society.

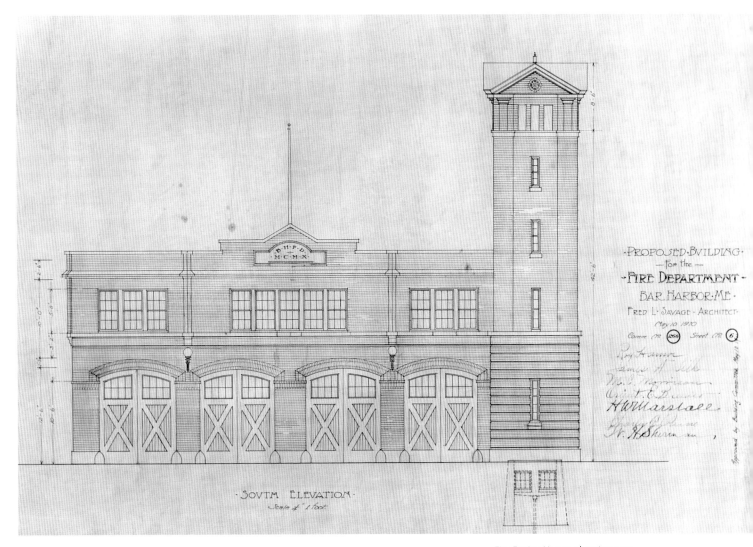

·SOVTH ELEVATION·
Scale ¼" 1 Foot

·PROPOSED·BVILDING·
— for the —
·FIRE DEPARTMENT·
BAR·HARBOR·ME·
FRED L· SAVAGE · ARCHITECT·
May 10 1910

Fire Engine House, elevation, 1911.
Courtesy of the Mount Desert Island
Historical Society.

231

The City Beautiful Movement in Bar Harbor

top: Building of Arts, Bar Harbor, Guy Lowell, 1907. Courtesy of the Bar Harbor Historical Society.

bottom: Jesup Library, Bar Harbor, William A. Delano, 1905. Courtesy of the Bar Harbor Historical Society.

These civic improvements coincided with the decline of cottage construction in Bar Harbor. No longer taking prosperity for granted, people committed to the community tried to burnish its image by providing new public facilities and otherwise improving the city's appearance. In 1908 Savage served as chairman of a committee of the Bar Harbor Board of Trade—the Chamber of Commerce of the day—charged with advertising the city as a resort; surviving correspondence suggests that he worked in this capacity until 1916. To help the tourist industry, Savage wrote railroads urging them to extend their summer schedules, and the Board of Trade asked hotel owners to add more than two months to the tourist season by opening in May and staying open until October. Savage also helped develop pamphlets promoting Bar Harbor.[46]

A draft of a promotional pamphlet among his papers praises one of the town's major new attractions:

> The Building of Arts, placed on an elevation looking southward through the mountain gap which opens a direct and striking way from Bar Harbor to the ocean front. Carefully planned by a committee of summer residents, who sought especially an ideal home for music and a background for the performance of world-famous artists who frequent the Island, it is a perfect example of Greek architecture that might appropriately crown the Acropolis or look down upon the groves of Mount Parnassus.... But five minutes' walk from one of Bar Harbor's gayest and most crowded centers of fashionable hotel life, no house is visible from the Building site, but only woods and mountains, and the broad golf lawns; and when mountain shadows lengthen over these, as one lingers after beautiful and noble music, the scene is one which leaves a deep impression.[47]

The Building of Arts (1907) was designed by Guy Lowell (1870–1927), a prominent Boston architect known for the classical balance and dignity of his work, and sponsored by George Washington Vanderbilt, George B. Dorr, Henry Lane Eno, Mrs. Robert Abbe, and Mrs. Henry Dimock. They hoped the building would "crystallize the diverse elements that form the summer colony into a real society, having as its objective the highest esthetic and intellectual stimulation . . . to contribute to self-education and the helpful mingling of city and village life."[48]

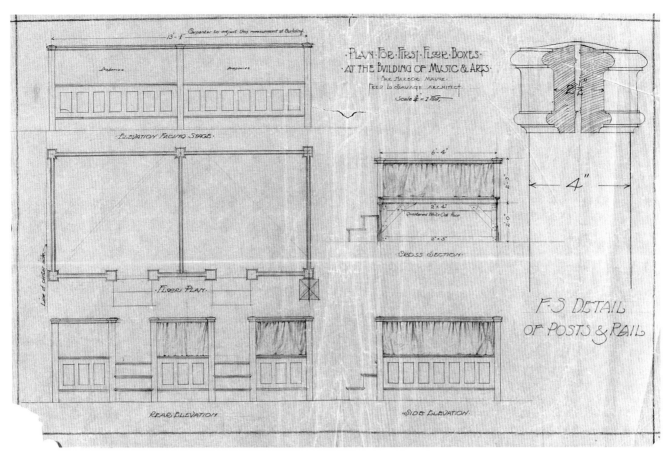

Like the Building of Arts, Bar Harbor's new library (1905) is singled out in the
draft pamphlet as an attraction,

> given to Bar Harbor... by Mrs. Morris K. Jesup, of New York, in memory of her
> husband and their long association with the Island's summer life. It is a joy to
> all who seek a quiet and studious spot in which to read or work.... A beautiful
> old-fashioned perennial garden surrounds the building on three sides... an
> interesting loan exhibition of etchings, prints and similar art objects.[49]

George Dorr (1853–1944), a wealthy Bostonian and lifelong seasonal resident of
Bar Harbor, is credited with suggesting to the widowed Mrs. Jesup that she fund the
library as a memorial. The building committee consisted of Dorr, Mrs. Jesup, Ernesto
Fabbri, and Henry Lane Eno, all cottagers. They selected William A. Delano
(1874–1960) of New York as their architect, and he produced a functional, elegant plan
of notable dignity given its compact scale. The entry leads into a domed rotunda with
specialized reading rooms to the left (originally for periodicals) and right (horticul-
ture), and the two-story, alcove-lined main reading room beyond.

The summer people responsible for the Jesup Library and the Building of Arts
would have known that their efforts were part of a nationwide citizens' movement to
create cultural attractions. The City Beautiful Movement (circa 1892–1915) grew out of
the success of the Olmsted plan for the grounds of the Columbian Exposition—the
Chicago World's Fair (1892–1893)—spawning civic associations that sponsored parks,
fountains, statues, and urban improvement projects from coast to coast. City Beautiful
enthusiasts did not typically advocate beauty for its own sake; instead, they promoted
amenities as a means of improving the psychological, educational, physical, and financial well-being of their communities.[50]

Savage served on two committees that promoted a City Beautiful plan designed for Bar Harbor by Beatrix Farrand (1872–1959) in 1919. Farrand, a distinguished landscape architect, second-generation summer resident, and owner of Reef Point cottage on the Shore Path, presented her plan under the auspices of the Bar Harbor Village Improvement Association to a public meeting at the YWCA on March 25, 1919. Savage was present as a member of the association's committee on resolutions. Calling her plan "Beautiful Bar Harbor," Farrand gave a lecture with slides depicting before and after views of economical ways to improve the waterfront and business district. She recommended "covering the sides of certain buildings with lattice work, the placing of window boxes in many windows, the shutting off of other ugly looking views by the use of latticed screens and the making of a pavilion between the Fifield & Joy store and the old bowling alleys." The audience was enthusiastic, and the following week a group of property owners—including Savage—met with the Bar Harbor selectmen, and Farrand presented her plan again. As a result of this second meeting a committee, consisting of Farrand and Savage, a Miss Baker, Mrs. W. E. Patterson, Clarence Dow, John H. Stalford, and Frank McGouldrick, was formed to implement the plan. The committee must not have been a success, however, since nothing is known about their accomplishments.[51]

The efforts to preserve the landscape and to make Bar Harbor attractive did not reverse the decline of the cottage era. After 1910 most of Savage's architectural work consisted of the design and management of alterations and additions rather than the creation of new cottages, with the exception of High Seas, his last major cottage.

Eagle Lake, Acadia National Park

High Seas (1911–1912)

above and opposite: High Seas, Bar Harbor, Fred L. Savage, 1912

Savage designed High Seas for Rudolph E. Brunnow (1858–1917), an internationally known scholar of Semitic languages—Arabic, Hebrew, Syriac, Ethiopic, and Assyrian. At first glance, his cottage, perched at the outmost edge of a narrow plateau on the steep eastern face of Champlain Mountain, appears ill-suited to its site. Immediately behind the house the cliff tumbles into the sea, and the formality of the cottage's colonial revival plan and elevations seem out of place in this dramatic setting. Taking into account Brunnow's background, however, the juxtaposition made sense and embodied the owner's interests.

Elite groups in western culture had long created carefully designed rural retreats where they could savor the fruits of culture in a natural setting. The Roman villas praised by Marcus Porcius Cato, the Italian villas designed by Andrea Palladio, the manor houses of the English aristocracy, and Jefferson's Monticello all used rustic or agrarian settings as a foil to emphasize urbanity. Brunnow must have seen the contrast between High Seas and its setting as part of this tradition. He was educated in Basel, Tubingen, and Strassburg, and thus would have known the famous German castles—Godesburg, Königswinter, Drachenburg, Drachenfels, and others—that were perched above the Rhine like High Seas is on its precipice above Frenchman's Bay.

High Seas's large library with its glazed bookcases suggests that Brunnow meant to pursue his intellectual interests on Mount Desert, but he was not a sedentary bookworm. Serving as chairman of the Path Committee of the Bar Harbor Village Improvement Association, he designed the Ladder Trail on Dorr Mountain, the Precipice Trail on Champlain Mountain, the Jordan Cliffs Trail, the Goat Trail on Pemetic, and the Shore Path southwest of Hunters Beach. His trails are notable for the use of iron pins, staples, and ladders, installed by local craftsmen directed by Brunnow and Dorr to make cliffs and vistas accessible to hardy hikers.[52]

High Seas's plan, with its twenty-three rooms, a servants' wing with five bedrooms, and a bath above the kitchen and pantry, indicates that the house, like Brunnow's trails, was meant to be shared. Like other large cottages, it was essentially a small hotel.

High Seas was one of the last large cottages built on Mount Desert during the final phase of the evolution of tourism as described by Godkin (see p. 269, note 9). Savage had participated as boardinghouses had given way to hotels, which in turn had been socially overshadowed by elaborate cottages. As the cottage era declined (long before the Great Depression and the fire of 1947), the creation of Acadia National Park

above and opposite: High Seas, Bar
Harbor, Fred L. Savage, 1912

and the coming of the automobile began to change the nature of tourism in ways that
Godkin could not have anticipated, as transient tourists in automobiles made the
summer landscape less tranquil and more democratic. Savage did not participate in the
movement to create the national park, but as soon as cars became legal on Bar Harbor
roads, he took the opportunity to supplement his income by becoming an agent for the
Franklin Automobile Company.

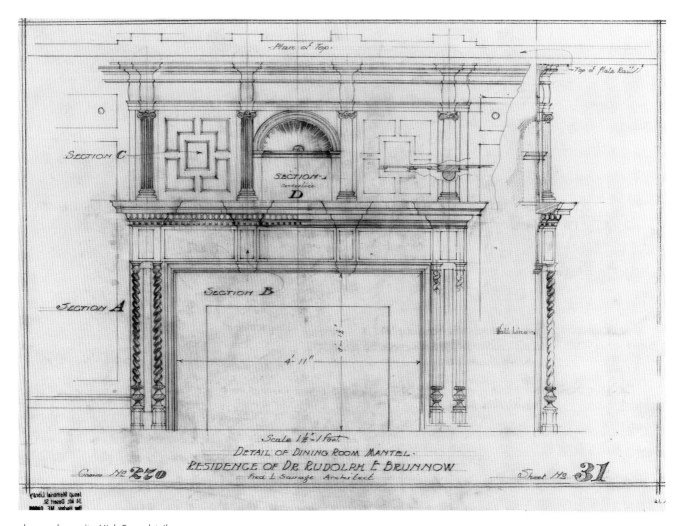

above and opposite: High Seas, details,
1912. Courtesy of the Mount Desert
Island Historical Society

DINING ROOM MANTLE SECTIO

241

Fred L. Savage, Automobile Dealer

Savage applied for the position as a sales agent for the car manufacturer although he knew that his principal clients would be displeased. In 1905 the cottage owners, feeling that cars would diminish the beauty and tranquility of Mount Desert, had lobbied as a block and successfully prevented the use of automobiles on the island. As nonresidents, cottagers could not vote at town meetings, but through personal contacts, newspaper articles, and a published poll, they convinced residents to impose and maintain the ban, until Bar Harbor voters repealed their anti-automobile ordinance in 1913.[53]

Savage must have seen the repeal coming; within weeks he became an authorized Franklin Automobile dealer for Hancock, Aroostook, and Washington counties. By acting decisively, he positioned himself to ride a new wave just as his ancestors had shifted from fishing for mackerel to pressing porgies, from cutting timber to quarrying granite, and finally from coasting to taking in rusticators.

Buildings and drawings provide tangible evidence of Savage's role in the early development of Mount Desert, but only newspaper accounts survive to convey his response to the early public interest in automobiles. Prior to World War I, automobile trips were still newsworthy. George W. Guthrie, a Bar Harbor cottager, drove three thousand miles across Europe, and on his return suggested the experience qualified him to declare Mount Desert unsuitable for cars.[54] Five years before cars were legal in Bar Harbor, three local boys—Leslie Brewer, Freddy Richardson, and Willie Dolliver—built a car using sulky wheels, a gasoline boat engine, and "an old circular saw [as] a friction gear whose power is increased or diminished . . . by drawing it from the center of the mechanism." Their maiden voyage was noted with praise as far away as Bangor.[55] Beginning in 1914, the press reported the number of cars in town, the condition of the roads, and automobile accidents. Cars fitted for camping were especially noteworthy.

The first "recreational vehicle" arrived in Bar Harbor in 1914. It was owned by an Englishman, Arthur Delroy, who was touring America, camping on hotel lawns, showing his car, and putting on performances that included magic tricks, hypnotism, and mind-reading. Delroy's car was equipped to provide "all the hotel conveniences" including two Pullman beds, a folding table, a collapsible bathtub, two folding hand basins (one for Delroy and another for the chauffeur), a kitchenette, an office, fishing tackle, tool kit, ice box, and "jiffy curtains, behind which are brown silk window blinds arranged in the manner of an up-to-date yacht cabin."[56]

Fred L. Savage at the wheel of a Franklin,
c. 1915. His office is in the background.
Courtesy of Ann Savage and Rose P. Ruze.

Savage's work as a Franklin agent involved publishing articles in which he praised Franklin cars, and his writings express the energy, pragmatism, and clarity that made his ventures successful; he also took trips to demonstrate the virtues of the Franklin cars, which were expensive. Savage advertised models costing up to $2,800 when a Ford could be purchased for $350, but the Franklin had a reputation for reliability and low operating costs.[57] Its use of an air-cooled engine simultaneously eliminated the radiator and water pump and allowed the engine to run 150 degrees hotter than a comparable water-cooled engine. Savage wrote that "this higher temperature means a greater expansive force in the gas; less gas is taken into the cylinders for one charge," which resulted in 20 to 35 percent better gas mileage than its competitors. The Franklin's body was also lighter and more flexible than others in its class, so "the Franklin owner gets FIVE TIMES the tire service per dollar of cost."[58]

The *Bar Harbor Times* published accounts of two test drives Savage made in 1914 and 1915, both to advertise the Franklin air-cooled engine. In September 1914,

> Fred Savage made his all day run on low gear in his Franklin car on Thursday without a mishap and covered 132 miles in ten hours on 14 gallons of gasoline and two quarts of lubricating oil.
>
> Without a thing going wrong, Mr. Savage drove his car to Castine, circled the village and came back—making his start at 8 o'clock in the morning and getting back at 6 at night. He was just two minutes later in arriving at Castine than he had laid out in his schedule and half an hour later in getting back to Bar Harbor because of having to make a detour around by the coast at Bluehill, as the other road was closed for repairs. This added four miles to his itinerary which altogether was 112 miles. The engine was running all the time and the test was made to show the advantage of the Franklin air cooled system. Mr. Savage had issued a challenge to any water cooled car to follow him, but none accepted. The route was chosen because it is acknowledged to be the hardest for the distance in Hancock county. . . .
>
> Interest was attracted all along the way. Chief of Police Gerry and Judge E. N. Benson accompanied Mr. Savage, and Mr. Savage's son, Francis, of Brewer, assisted in driving.[59]

Fred L. Savage, Dealer, *Bar Harbor Record*, June 17, 1914.

Or again:

Remarkable Winter Spin

Mr. And Mrs. Fred L. Savage motored from Bar Harbor to Machias and returned on Wednesday last, covering a distance of 170 miles at an average speed of 19 miles per hour for the entire trip. Mr. Savage says the roads on the whole are in remarkably good condition for motoring except that from Franklin to Cherryfield, a distance of about 15 miles, no motors have passed through this month and there was only the marks of narrow sleds and sleighs which are much too narrow for the gauge of a motor car. He therefore had to plough through about ten inches of snow having a top crust hard and strong enough to bear the weight of a 200 pound man. This distance of 15 miles was run in one hour, all on the low gear. Mr. Savage estimates that in the most difficult place on the hills his motor must have been turning up to the tune of nearly 2,000 revolutions per minute on account of the rear wheels spinning in the snow. However the engine seemed to enjoy the music and the car just waltzed along in the good old fashioned way without any hesitating. Mr. and Mrs. Savage made their entire trip in their Franklin air cooled car.[60]

The Twilight of Savage's Architectural Career

Architectural work grew scarce on Mount Desert as World War I approached, and this decline probably played a role in Savage's decision to sell cars. The golden age of cottage construction was over, and he received no more commissions on the scale of High Seas. Nonetheless, he remained active as an architect and designed additions and alterations for a series of existing cottages in Bar Harbor including Chiltern (1914), Hauterive (1915), Tanglewold (1915–1917), and the Malvern Hotel (1915). He also designed the C. L. Morang store in Bar Harbor (1912), a naval radio facility at Otter Cliffs (1917), and two institutional buildings—the Bar Harbor Isolated Hospital (1913) and the Northeast Harbor Stetson Grammar School (1915). He prepared plans for the Islesford Inn (1915) to replace one that had burned and directed the reconstruction of Buonriposa (1918), a Bar Harbor cottage that had burned, using plans prepared or provided by the owner, Ernesto Fabbri.[61]

It is poetically fitting that Savage's final commission was a large automobile garage at Hauterive, a Bar Harbor cottage owned by Josephine E. Carpenter. The construction was almost completed when he died suddenly on February 26, 1924. (Hauterive burned around 1922; only Savage's garage survives.)

C. L. Morang Store, Bar Harbor,
Fred L. Savage, 1912

The Hauterive Garage (1921–1924)

Like Savage's career, Hauterive cottage was transformed by the shift from the
shingle style to the more formal historical revival styles. William Ralph Emerson
had designed two shingle-style cottages at Hauterive in 1881 and 1886 for Samuel
E. Lyons and his son-in-law, General William A. Smith. The property, which was then
called Edenfield, was purchased in 1899 by Mrs. Carpenter. She had one of the
cottages remodeled in the Tudor revival style by Andrews, Jacques & Rantoul, and
renamed it Hauterive for its site on a high bank above Frenchman's Bay.[62] The
cottage's interiors were ornate, while its porches and grounds reflected the cottagers'
interest in being out-of-doors. Mrs. Carpenter's great-niece, Josephine Morrison,
described the interior of the house in notes accompanying a photograph album
of Hauterive:

> One entered Hauterive by a large hall, which opened at the opposite end on to a
> porch, with a wonderful view of the Bay, as had most of the windows throughout the
> house. This hall was panelled in dark wood, and had a large fire place, where big
> birch logs would snap and spark in the Autumn.
>
> On one wall were large sepia photographs in heavy frames of the Italian
> masters admired by the Pre-Raphaelites. There was also an oak bookcase, a copy of
> mediaeval carving, containing books about the Pre-Raphaelite art, which remained
> *in situ* as long as Hauterive stood, making a quiet cultural corner of American life
> strongly influenced by Pre-Raphaelitism.
>
> On the right of the hall was a delicately and lightly decorated drawing room
> furnished in the French 18th century style by Duveen. On the left of the hall, was a
> large staircase, a small boudoir with similar pretty furniture, and beyond a large
> dining room, decorated latterly by Baron de Meyer, which had a green-grey carpet
> and red lacquered furniture.
>
> Upstairs were seven bedrooms, together with rooms for six servants, and the
> wonderful view.[63]

The Carpenters counted the Aldrichs, Rockefellers, and Macys among
their friends, and although Savage rarely created whole cottages for the wealthiest
summer people, he often designed alterations, additions, and outbuildings for
them as he did at Hauterive. His design for the garage called for the same foundation
of cobbles with Tudor revival stucco and half-timbering above that he had used

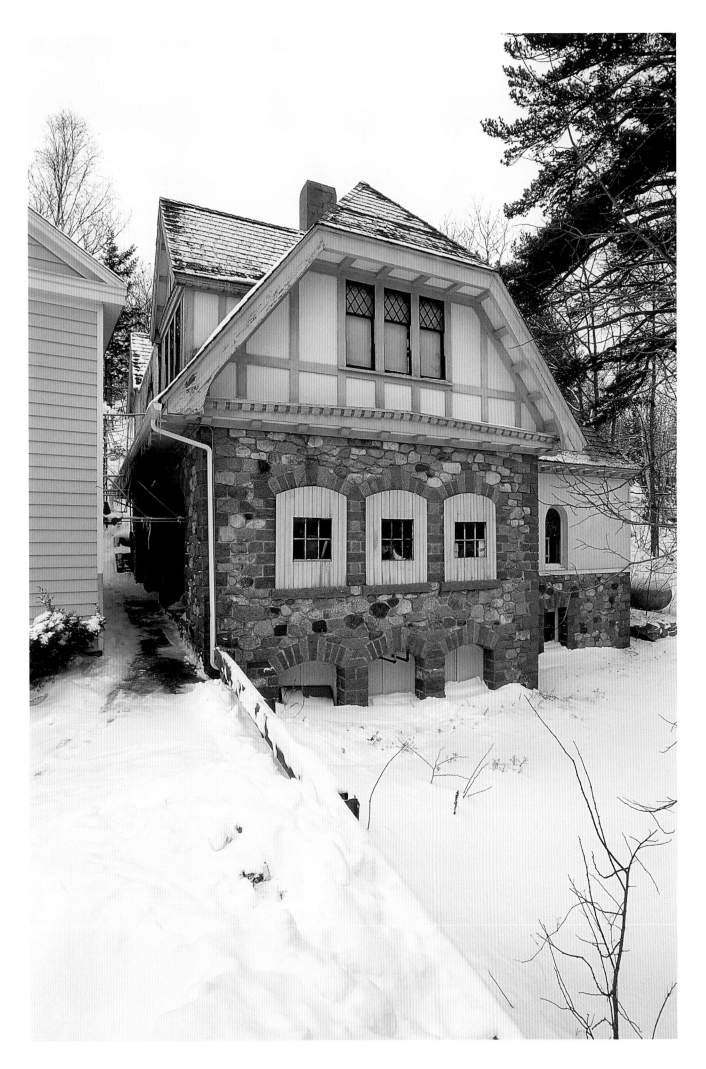

at the Atlantean, Devilstone, and Breakwater cottages and the West Gouldsboro Library. The garage was his second project at Hauterive; in 1915 he had designed a Tudor revival service wing containing a servants' dining room, a butler's room, spare room, and baths, much as he had done at Devilstone and Mossley Hall.[64]

The Hauterive photo album, which contains more than three hundred images and spans the years between 1899 and 1941, preserves an evocative record of the link between style and life-style in Bar Harbor during the twilight of the cottage era. The Carpenter family personifies Savage's primary clientele, and their album shows them decorously enjoying the grounds and porches of Hauterive. Here we glimpse a life of privilege played out upon a stage set by Savage and his peers. As Morrison's notes in the album state, "Mrs. Carpenter and her daughter Agnes went every year to Paris to buy clothes, to travel and to take a cure at Karlsbad, returning to Hauterive in June for the summer and to the life of comfort and luxury of a past era."[65] At first glance, everything at Hauterive appears alien to the simplicity sought by the early rusticators, but these cottagers, like the artists and rusticators who preceded them, were drawn by the enduring natural drama of Mount Desert. Being outside was of primary importance to the Carpenter family in their summers at Hauterive, as Morrison's notes reveal:

> The porch which we now would term a "Terrace," ran alongside the whole length of the house; outside the drawing room was a space for sitting, and outside the dining room was a table for meals.

Large jars at the edge of the porch were planted with flowers at which humming birds would flutter in spite of Bar Harbor being so far north.

The lawn sloped down to the balustrade above the Bay; to the right was another lawn with a semicircle of marble seats, and a rose garden with brick paths which ended by a fountain where one had afternoon tea, and which could be called the summer parlor.[66]

Savage's Estate

When Savage died at the age of sixty-three in February 1924, he was survived by his second wife, Alice Preble Savage, and his two children, Francis Chase Savage and Floralee Savage. Fred L. Savage's possessions were divided among his family according to his will, which he had prepared on October 20, 1914. He divided his real estate between his son and his daughter, while Alice Preble Savage was named executrix and inherited all the personal property. The estate inventory listed four lots (the Atlantean and Vista Cottage parcel, a one-fifth common interest in the Northeast Harbor land remaining in the A. C. Savage estate, and two inland lots in the town of Hancock, Maine).[67]

Several entries in the probate documents are especially interesting. For example, after Savage's death, his widow received payment for "plans sold Mrs. Hastings, $500," "plans sold Mrs. King, $150," "plans sold Mrs. Hawkes, $100," and "plans sold Samuel Fells, $331.40," and this list is our best indication of what Savage charged for architectural plans. A total of $3,000 was received by the estate as rent for the Atlantean for the 1924 and 1925 seasons; it had also been rented for the 1906 season, and Savage probably built it with this in mind. Miss Agnes Carpenter paid the estate $7,100 to settle the amount owed Savage for work on the Hauterive garage.

Claims against the estate show that Savage maintained accounts with contractors and suppliers. When he died, everyone working on the Hauterive garage turned to his widow to settle their accounts: F. J. Brewer & Son, electrical contractors, submitted a bill as well as John W. Silk & Son, plumbers; William L. Pierce, plumber; Shea Brothers, masonry contractors; and Morse & Company of Bangor, suppliers of lumber, hardware, and paint. The Franklin Motor Car Company also submitted a bill for $635.71. Their invoice shows that Savage had sold four cars in 1922. When the estate was settled on July 20, 1926, Alice Preble Savage received $1,479.72.[68]

Otter Point, Acadia National Park

A Postscript

As an architect, Fred L. Savage was in the right place at the right time. Family-owned land, fortuitous training, and the timing of the cottage era all launched and sustained his career. He died as the initial burst of development was fading, but he had lived long enough to see the beginnings of the conservation movement and the coming of automobiles—two forces that will affect life on Mount Desert for the foreseeable future. Approximately seventy-five of his buildings survive in various stages of preservation, and his work, like that of many of Savage's peers, has recently benefited from both a new civic awareness of historic preservation as an aspect of tourism and a revival of interest in the shingle style. In recent years several architects, including Roc R. Caivano and Robert A. M. Stern, have created shingle-style buildings on Mount Desert that are in harmony with Savage's early work.

For twenty-five years following Savage's death in 1924, the world war and the Great Depression stifled tourism; then, almost as a *coup de grace*, on October 17 to November 7, 1947, a forest fire swept across the eastern side of Mount Desert, burning 17,188 acres and destroying 67 of 122 summer cottages and 170 of 667 year-round homes in Bar Harbor. When the tourist industry began to revive in the 1950s, it was based on an ever-increasing stream of short-term visitors traveling in privately owned automobiles. Most of them came—and still come—to experience Acadia National Park. During July and August, up to fourteen thousand people a day cross the causeway leading onto Mount Desert. With three million annual visitors, Acadia has become one of our most heavily used parks, and the number of mobile tourists has affected many aspects of the island.

In his 1904 pamphlet (see page 216), President Eliot noted that different types of tourists need different services. He also observed that public policies on the island should balance the interests of year-round residents with the conservation of the landscape and facilities to nurture a diversified tourist population. Today life on the island is influenced by competition between the various needs of year-round residents, seasonal or long-term summer residents, transitory tourists, and the range of commercial and public resources they require or desire. The rivalry between these divergent interests is magnified by the success of the conservation effort (the park contains almost a third of the island, or 45,000 acres, and conservation easements have been placed on another 170 parcels of privately owned land). Squeezed between preserved landscape and the sea, there is little space available for development; consequently, land and home prices have soared, and many working families find it difficult or impossible to live on the island. The median home price on Mount Desert in 2003 was $265,000, an increase of 83 percent from 2000 (as compared to a median price of $109,900 for the state as a whole and a 2000–2003 increase of 36 percent).

Many lifelong residents of Northeast Harbor claim that the cost of housing has killed Savage's hometown as a year-round community.[69] The few remaining year-round families typically drive fifteen miles to shop in national chain stores in Ellsworth, the nearest sizable town on the mainland. After the summer people leave, there is thus no longer enough retail business to support a pharmacy or dentist or grocery store. Throughout the winter, most of the storefronts are dark and shuttered. In summertime, on the other hand, there are several art galleries along Main Street—all in stores that formerly sold hardware, thread, soap, and other mundane but necessary merchandise.

The impact of automobile-based tourism is evident all over the island. Acadia National Park is famous for its network of more than one hundred named trails (totaling 150 miles) and 75 miles of carriage roads (for horses, hikers, and bicyclists) and scenic roads accessible to automobiles. The carriage road system (circa 1915–1933) was funded by John D. Rockefeller, Jr., and includes seventeen stone bridges by the architect Grosvenor Atterbury. The volume of traffic has necessitated the development of parking areas, rest rooms, guardrails, designated swimming areas, and beach access points. To accommodate campers there are 530 tent sites within the park and 1,730 more tent sites in private campgrounds on the island. In Bar Harbor, the hotels of Savage's day have been replaced by motels and inns that together can accommodate as many as eight thousand guests per night. During the last decade, the Chamber of Commerce effectively promoted Bar Harbor as a port of call for coastal and international cruise ships and a significant numbers of tourists have been arriving by sea as they did a century ago. Only four ships stopped in Bar Harbor in 1990, but in 2004 twenty different ships, varying in size from the *American Glory* (49 passengers) to the *Queen Mary 2* (2,620 passengers), made a total of eighty-seven visits. Most dock for a day; this revival of the way almost everyone once arrived brings thousands of visitors to walk around and shop in Bar Harbor.

Growth and efforts to influence it create problems. This is especially true in a place as finite, popular, and environmentally sensitive as Mount Desert. It is heartening to note that organizations are now working together to balance the various interests articulated by President Eliot. Citizens' organizations like Mount Desert Island Tomorrow and Friends of Acadia are currently addressing a broad array of issues, including affordable housing, water quality and solid waste management, community health, programs for young people, diversification of the economy, and transportation.

The pressures created by development will not go away, for the enduring beauty of Mount Desert and its environs will continue to draw millions. Nonetheless, many people appreciate the island, and with various groups working together, there is reason to hope a balance can be struck between growth and preservation. I am hopeful and enjoy the thought of future generations on porches savoring lilacs, balsam, and salt air.

Notes

Acknowledgments

1   Charles W. Eliot, "John Gilley, Maine Farmer and Fisherman," Charles W. Eliot, *A Man and His Beliefs*, William Allen Neilson, ed. (New York: Harper & Brothers, 1926), 439.

Introduction

1   The 1880 U.S. Census notes that Fred L. Savage was born in 1862; family records indicate that he was born on November 14, 1861. 1880 U.S. Census, Family History Library, National Archives, Film # 1254480, NA Film Number T9-0480, page 363D; also see: Emily Phillips Reynolds, "My Recollections of Grandfather and Grandmother and Their Family" (1982), Northeast Harbor Library.

2   *The Mount Desert Herald*, October 31, 1884; also see *The Industrial Journal*, February 18, 1887; also see note 33 below. Two articles have been published about Savage's life and work: Jaylene B. Roths, "Fred Savage, the Cottage Builder," *The History Journal of the Mount Desert Historical Society* II (1999): 38–56; and Letitia Baldwin, "Savage Beauties, the Summer Palaces of Frederick L. Savage," *Downeast* (February 1996): 32–37.

3   Appendix I, a preliminary list of buildings by Savage, provides an overview of his career; it is based on the architectural drawings saved by Lewis E. Gerrish. The drawings are now in collections of the Northeast Harbor Library and the Mount Desert Historical Society. Architectural surveys conducted in 1984 and 1985 by T. Mark Cole for the Maine Historic Preservation Commission and Roger G. Reed's "Bar Harbor Cottages, 1868–1940, A List of Summer Cottages with Architects and Builders" (Fall 1988, revised February 1992), typescript, also sponsored by the Maine Historic Preservation Commission (Augusta, Maine) establish the context of Savage's life and work. Approximately three thousand drawings and seventy-five buildings by Savage survive.

Chapter I

1   Sarah Dolibar was variously spelled at the time as Dolibar, Dolliver, Dolivar, or Doliber.

2   Gunnar Hansen, ed., *Mount Desert, an Informal History* (Mount Desert: The Town of Mount Desert, 1989), 42.

3   Richard Walden Hale, Jr., *The Story of Bar Harbor* (New York: Ives Washburn, 1949), 77–78.

4   Augustus Chase Savage, "Memories of a Lifetime," typescript, 1902. I am grateful to Sam McGee and Rick Savage, descendants of A. C. Savage, for providing copies of the memoir.

5   In each generation active members of the Savage family were open to change, a tendency manifest here in architecture, but also seen later in a series of progressive business ventures. Coasting allowed John II and his son A. C. to see many communities along the Atlantic seaboard, but whatever the reason, the Savages never adhered to the classically based Federal and Greek revival styles the way most of their neighbors up the sound in Somesville did.

6   For more than a century, long-term seasonal visitors to Maine have been called *rusticators* by local residents. *The Oxford English Dictionary* defines *rustic* as "of or pertaining to the country as opposed to

the town," and *to rusticate* as "to stay or sojourn in the country; to assume rural manners; to live a country life." The term is still used; see John N. Cole, "Dreams of Rustication," *Maine Times* (October 4, 2001), 27.

7   The first known family to stay at Asticou must have been that of Joseph P. Fyffe (1832–1896). During the James River campaign of 1864, as a U.S. Navy Lieutenant, Fyffe destroyed Confederate batteries at Deep Bottom using cannons mounted on the *U.S.S. Hunchback*, a converted ferry. He may have sought A. C. Savage to reminisce as ex-comrades in arms. "Brown" may have been W. Warren Brown (active 1887) or Harrison Bird Brown (1831–1915). "Hollingsworth" was probably George Hollingsworth (1813–1882).

8   Along the coast of Maine the term *cottage* has long been used to denote a summer residence; the term *house* usually implies year-round use, and the term *camp* signifies a seasonal residence with little or no interior finish. See Samuel Eliot Morison, *The Story of Mount Desert Island, Maine* (Boston: Little, Brown, 1960), 50.

9   Edwin Lawrence Godkin, "The Evolution of a Summer Resort," reprinted in Charles and Samuella Shain, eds., *The Maine Reader* (Boston: Houghton Mifflin, 1991), 351–356. Using Bar Harbor as his principal example, Godkin defines three phases of development as being typical of American resorts; his focus is on the progressive loss of public access and the increasingly elaborate social rituals that accompany development. Godkin's turn-of-the-century analysis has been endorsed by subsequent writers; see, for example, G. W. Helfrich and Gladys O'Neil, *Lost Bar Harbor* (Camden: Down East Books, 1982), 2–3.

10   Roderick Nash, *Wilderness and the American Mind* (New Haven and London: Yale University Press, 1973), especially pages 8–22, 25–43.

11   John Winthrop, *Conclusions for the Plantation in New England* (629) in *Old South Leaflets* vol. 2, no. 50 (Boston, 1895): 5, as quoted by Nash, *Wilderness*, 31.

12   Ralph Waldo Emerson, "Nature," in *Nature, Addresses and Lectures, the Works of Ralph Waldo Emerson* I (Boston, 1883), 31, 38; Bradford Torrey and Francis H. Allen, eds., *Journal of Henry David Thoreau* V (Boston, 1906), 45, both as quoted by Nash, *Wilderness*, 85.

13   Quoted by Franklin Kelly, "Frederic Edwin Church and the North American Landscape, 1845–1860" (Ph.D. diss., University of Delaware, 1985), 105. For ideas presented by early landscape paintings in America see William H. Gerdts, "American Landscape Painting: Critical Judgments, 1730–1845," *The American Art Journal* vol. 5, no. 17 (Winter 1985): 28–59.

14   Kelly, *Frederic Edwin Church*, 105.

15   G. W. Curtis as quoted by Kelly, *Frederic Edwin Church*, 162.

16   William Cullen Bryant, ed., *Picturesque America; or, The Land We Live In* I (New York: D. Appleton and Co., 1872), 1–2, 10–11.

17   John Wilmerding, *The Artist's Mount Desert, American Painters on the Maine Coast* (Princeton: Princeton University Press, 1994); see also Pamela J. Belanger, *Inventing Acadia, Artists and Tourists at Mount Desert* (Rockland: The Farnsworth Art Museum, 1999). Both provide comprehensive, well illustrated accounts of the artists' critical role in the development of tourism on Mount Desert.

18   Quoted by William A. Koelsch, "Antebellum Harvard Students and the Recreational Exploration of the New England Landscape," *Journal of Historical Geography* vol. 8, no. 4 (1982): 365 and 367.

19   Henry James, *Charles W. Eliot, President of Harvard University, 1869–1909* vol. 1 (Boston: Houghton Mifflin, 1930), 54.

20   Henry David Thoreau, *The Maine Woods* (1864; reprint, New York: Bramhall House, 1950), 128.

21   Robert Carter, *Summer Cruise of the Coast of New England* (Boston: Crosby and Nichols, New York: Oliver S. Felt, 1864). Carter's account was published serially in the newspaper before it came out as a book. Bill and Kendra Cheney brought this book to my attention, and I am deeply grateful. The *Helen* was registered in Swampscott, May 7, 1858, as being thirty-two feet and seven inches long, twelve feet and five inches beam, five feet and two inches draught, and "to be employed in carrying on the cod-fishery," 8–9.

22   Ibid., 4.

23   Ibid., 11–12.

24   Ibid., 257–260.

25   Hale, *The Story of Bar Harbor*, 126. See also Belanger, *Inventing Acadia*, 44, note 15.

26   Hale, *The Story of Bar Harbor*, 128.

27   G. W. Helfrich and Gladys O'Neil, *Lost Bar Harbor* (Camden, Maine: Downeast Books, 1982), 5.

28   Ibid., 5, 7.

29   A. C. Savage recorded expenses weekly, and the accounts indicate that work began on Thuya Lodge on or about November 11, 1880. He "commenced work for Charles W. Eliot Esq" on March 29, 1881. The building accounts with Curtis seem to have been settled on October 14, 1882, and the Eliot building account is marked "settled" on May 26, 1883. *A. C. Savage*, a leather-bound journal in the collection of Rick Savage. The Eliot cottage has always been cited as the first in Northeast Harbor, but this cannot be true. Curtis seems to have been the first rusticator to settle in Northeast Harbor. No records are available to establish a date for the completion of the Doane cottage. I am grateful to Rick Savage for making the A. C. Savage account book available.

30   Charles W. Eliot, *Charles Eliot, Landscape Architect* (Amherst: University of Massachusetts Press, 1999), 9.

31   James notes that the summer of 1873 was spent camping on Nonamesset, adjacent Naushon Island south of Cape Cod. Eliot's chronology differs slightly from James's. See Eliot, *Charles Eliot*, 9. Henry James describes the camps as "small tent colonies. Eliot had one sleeping-tent of his own, the two boys another. There was a large dining-room tent, and several more tents were arranged for guests, for a kitchen, and for the necessary services. The yacht was usually moored close by. Its steward was then camp cook. Until the boys grew bigger, and when there were ladies in the party, there was usually a maid in camp. Eliot ran the commissariat, arranged and led exploring expeditions and picnics, and was, in short, skipper, shore commander, housekeeper, host, and organizer of entertainments." James, *Charles W. Eliot*, 321. He notes that the *Sunshine* was "one of the first American yachts designed especially for cruising along the New England Coast" and was built in the spring of 1872 by Albertson Brothers of Philadelphia. Ibid., 322.

32   The group of friends called themselves the Champlain Society. One of the campers, Nathaniel Southgate Shaler, published *The Geology of the Island of Mount Desert, Maine* (Washington: Government Printing Office, 1889), the earliest scientific explanation of Mount Desert's picturesque or sublime topography.

33   Emily Philips Reynolds (1889–1984) was the architect's niece, the daughter of his sister Cora Justina Savage Phillips.

34   This typescript (1982) is in the collection of the Northeast Harbor Library, 2; Gunnar Hansen, *Not a Common House, a History of St. Mary's-by-the-Sea* (Privately printed, 1981), 19.

35   Reynolds, *My Recollections of Grandfather and Grandmother*, unpaginated typescript, Northeast Harbor Library.

36   Henry W. Lawrence, "Southern Spas: Source of the American Resort Tradition," *Landscape* vol. 27 no. 2 (1983): 10.

37   The extensive literature on the development of American resorts includes: David W. Francis, "Cedar Point and the Characteristics of American Summer Resorts During the Gilded Age," *Hayes Historical Journal* vol. 7, no. 2 (1988): 5–27; Douglas W. McCombs, "Therapeutic Rusticity: Antimodernism, Health and the Wilderness Vacation, 1870–1915," *New York History* vol. 76, no. 4 (1995): 409–428; Nancy H. Ferguson, "The American Resort Hotel in the Nineteenth Century," *Historical New Hampshire* vol. 50, no. 1–2 (1995): 6–21; and Blair Bolling, E. Lee Shepard, eds., "'Trip to the Virginia Spring': an Extract from the Diary of Blair Bolling, 1838," *Virginia Magazine of History and Biography* vol. 96, no. 2 (1988): 193–212.

38   Very few of Fred Savage's personal papers survive, so it is impossible to establish exact dates for many of the pivotal events in his life. *The Mount Desert Herald*, October 31, 1884, reported he was in Boston studying with Peabody and Stearns, and *The Industrial Journal*, December 3, 1886, a newspaper published in Bangor, Maine, reported that "F. L. Savage is to build two cottages at Northeast Harbor, Mt. Desert, one for Lieut. Davenport (fig. 45) of Washington, D.C. and the other for himself." Six weeks later, changing tense, the same journal reported "Lieut. R. G. Davenport, U.S. Navy, is having built a handsome cottage at Northeast Harbor, Mount Desert, which he will occupy with his family the coming summer. Fred L. Savage, the architect of the Davenport cottage, is also building a fine cottage for himself there." February 18, 1887. Savage seems to have been back working in Northeast Harbor by the winter of 1886–1887.

39   Leland M. Roth, *Shingle Styles, Innovation and Tradition in American Architecture, 1874–1982* (New York: Harry N. Abrams, 1999), 29.

40 Vincent J. Scully, Jr. *The Shingle Style and the Stick Style: Architectural Theory and Design from Downing to the Origins of Wright* (New Haven: Yale University Press, 1955), 100. See also Scully, *The Shingle Style Today, or the Historian's Revenge* (New York: George Braziller, 1974).

41 Ibid.

42 Wheaton A. Holden, "The Peabody Touch: Peabody and Stearns of Boston, 1870–1917," *Journal of the Society of Architectural Historians* vol. 32, no. 2 (1973): 120. For Peabody's contributions to the colonial revival see William B. Rhoads, "The Discovery of America's Architectural Past, 1874–1914," *Studies in the History of Art* vol. 5, no. 35 (1990): 23–39.

43 Robert D. Andrews, *The Architectural Review* (November 1917), quoted by Holden, "The Peabody Touch," 115. Robert Day Andrews (1857–1928) went on to a successful career as a partner in the firms of Andrews, Jacques & Rantoul and then with Andrews, Jones, Biscoe & Whitmore.

44 Hubert G. Ripley, *Julius A. Schweinfurth, Designer and Master Draughtsman*, undated reminiscence, 2; quoted by Holden, "The Peabody Touch," 116.

45 Ripley, *Julius A. Schweinfurth*, as quoted by Holden, "The Peabody Touch," 116, note 7.

46 The church held Boston Unitarian services in the summer and Baptist services in the winter. Robert R. Pyle, conversation with the author, January 2003.

47 The Wedge, Savage's first cottage, survives, but it has been extensively altered. For concise discussions of Downing's contribution to the development of the American asymmetrical dwelling, see Scully, *The Shingle Style and the Stick Style*, xxiii–xlv; see also Scully, "American Houses: Thomas Jefferson to Frank Lloyd Wright," in Edgar Kaufmann, Jr., ed., *The Rise of an American Architecture* (New York: Praeger, 1970), 170.

48 For the rustic-style Putnam camp, see Craig Gilborn, *Adirondack Camps, Homes Away from Home, 1850–1950* (Syracuse: Syracuse University Press, 2000), 138–139. Vitruvius, *The Ten Books of Architecture* (New York, Dover, 1960), 38–39. For an illustration of Davis's rustic cottage see Amelia Peck, ed., *Alexander Jackson Davis, American Architect, 1803–1892* (New York: Rizzoli, 1992), 64, plate 3.6.

49 Marc-Antoine Abbé Laugiér, *Essai sur l'Architecture* (Paris: Chez Duichesne, 1758) and Sir William Chambers, *A Treatise on the Decorative Part of Civil Architecture* (London: Joseph Smeeton, 1791).

50 George F. Moffette, Jr., is listed in the Boston City Directories, 1872–1913. Massachusetts Committee for the Preservation of Architectural Records, comp., *Directory of Boston Architects, 1846–1970* (Cambridge: COPAR, 1984), 47. *The Boston Architecture Index*, Fine Arts Department, Boston Public Library, Boston, Mass., cites seven projects, all residential, by Moffette. He is listed as being thirty-five years old in the 1880 U.S. Census.

51 Katharine L. Savage, an untitled typescript, Northeast Harbor Library, 7.

52 As quoted by Gunnar Hansen, *Not a Common House* (privately printed, 1981), 6.

53 Drawings—but no other office records—from the office of Peabody and Stearns are in the collection of the Boston Public Library. Janice H. Chadbourne, curator of fine arts, notes that it is not possible to positively attribute drawings to individuals, for the drawings are unsigned. There are twenty-five drawings of the Union Church in the collection. Janice H. Chadbourne, conversation with the author, October, 21, 2002.

Chapter II

1 *Bar Harbor Record*, March 31, 1887.

2 *Mount Desert Herald*, Bar Harbor, April 20, 1888.

3 Fred L. Savage, Architect, Bar Harbor, Maine, *Attractive Summer Homes and Scenes* (Privately printed, c. 1903), Northeast Harbor Library.

4 I am grateful to Beth Whitney of Bar Harbor and Earle G. Shettleworth, Jr., for information about Milton W. Stratton. The project that brought Stratton to Bar Harbor has not been identified, and little is known about his career. The Maine Historic Preservation Commission, Augusta, Maine, maintains a file on Stratton.

5 For concise biographies of Savage's Maine-born peers see Earle G. Shettleworth, Jr., and Roger G. Reed, eds., *A Biographical Dictionary of Architects in Maine*, a serial publication by the Maine Historic Preservation Commission, 1984–present.

6 *Bar Harbor Record*, May 6, 1914; *Bar Harbor Times*, January 16, 1915.

7   Henry H. Saylor, *Journal of the American Institute of Architects, The AIA's First Hundred Years* (Washington: AIA, 1957), 3–6; Tony P. Wrenn, "A Purely Local Affair, A History of the AIA's Chapters," *AIA Architect* (October 1999): 22–23. Kimberly J. Baker-Stetson of the Maine Board of Licensure kindly provided data about architectural licensing in Maine.

8   Some of the project rolls contain forty or fifty drawings; other rolls only contain two or three. In addition to the project rolls, there are some forty loose, unidentified drawings.

9   The commission number does not appear on all of the drawings, and given the current state of the surviving drawings, a complete, chronological list of projects cannot be compiled at this time.

10   In an article in the *Bar Harbor Times*, August 8, 1914, "News and Facts of General Interest to all Automobilists," Savage says he can be found at 17 Cottage Street—presumably the address of his office.

11   Agnes E. Platt to Fred L. Savage, undated typescript, Mount Desert Historical Society. Town of Mount Desert, Maine.

12   Draftsmen or assistants who worked for Savage are known only through brief notices in the newspaper, and the references usually state only their arrival or departure; we cannot determine how long each one stayed. For George Augustus Savage see the *Bar Harbor Times*, March 25, 1896; for Fred C. Watson, see the *Bar Harbor Record*, October 4, 1905; for Thurlow Workman and Arthur Stanley, see the *Bar Harbor Record*, May 15, 1907 and July 17, 1907, respectively. For William G. Bunker, see the *Bar Harbor Record*, January 1, 1913; and for Louis E. Jackson, see the *Bar Harbor Record*, December 15, 1915.

13   Henry F. and Elsie R. Withey, *Biographical Dictionary of American Architects (Deceased)* (Los Angeles: Hennessey & Ingalls, 1970), 318.

14   Vincent J. Scully, Jr., "The Cottage Style, an Organic Development in Later 19th Century Wooden Domestic Architecture in the Eastern United States" (Ph.D. diss., Yale University, 1949).

15   Scully, *The Shingle Style and the Stick Style*, 71–90.

16   Scully, *The Shingle Style and the Stick Style*, 83–88. See also Scully, Introduction to *The Architecture of the American Summer, The Flowering of the Shingle Style* (New York: Rizzoli, 1989), 1–11.

17   Maria G. van Rensselaer, "American Country Dwellings," *The Century Magazine*, vol. XXXII (June 1886): 209–210, quoted by Roger G. Reed, *A Delight to All Who Know It, The Maine Summer Architecture of William R. Emerson* (Portland, Maine: Maine Citizens for Historic Preservation, 1995), 11.

18   Quoted by Reed, *A Delight to All Who Know It*, 15; see also page 23, note 17.

19   For illustrations see Helfrich and O'Neil, *Lost Bar Harbor*, 40, 28, and 27.

20   Nathan Rosenberg, ed., *The American System of Manufactures* (Edinburgh: University of Edinburgh Press, 1969), 343–344.

21   Brooke Hindle, ed., *America's Wooden Age: Aspects of Its Early Technology* (Tarrytown: Sleepy Hollow Restorations, 1985), 78.

22   Their names were William A. Jordan, Suminsby and Dole, Richard Hamoor, J. C. Doane, Stephen Higgins, Walter W. Doane, Ambrose Higgins, Jordan and Clark, and Howard Marshall. This review of the contractors and architects who participated in the development of Bar Harbor is based upon the typescript "Bar Harbor Cottages, 1868–1940, a List of Summer Cottages with Architects and Builders," prepared by Roger G. Reed for the Maine Historic Preservation Commission (Fall 1988, revised February 1992). I am grateful to Earle G. Shettleworth, Jr., for providing access to this data.

23   See Appendix I.

24   Reynolds, "My Recollections of Grandfather," 2. Reynolds was mistaken. The towers were erected by Joseph H. Curtis. Robert R. Pyle to the author, January 2003.

25   Dr. Caspar Morris was also a member of the Philadelphia and University Clubs. *New York Times*, March 2, 1944.

26   *Mount Desert Herald*, April 18, 1889.

27   H. W. Cleaveland, W. Backus, and S. D. Backus, *Village and Farm Cottages: The requirements of American village homes considered and suggested; with designs for such houses of moderate cost* (New York: D. Appleton, 1856), 91–92.

28   Clara Barnes Martin, *The New York Transcript* [1866], a collection of undated clippings in the collection of the Northeast Harbor Library, 13–14. Due to growing public interest in Mount Desert, Martin's articles were published as a book, *Mount Desert, on the Coast of Maine* (Portland: B. Thurston, 1867), which was reissued in 1870, 1874, 1877, 1880, and 1885.

29   B. F. DeCosta, *Rambles in Mount Desert* (New York: A.D.Fl. Randolph & Co., 1871), 11; M. F. Sweetser, *Chisholm's Mount-Desert Guide-Book* (Portland: Chisholm Brothers, 1888), 39, 47, 28.

30   W. B. Lapham, *Bar Harbor and Mount Desert Island* (Bar Harbor, Maine, n.p., 1887), 13. Wiswell's first name varies in the documents.

31   Most cottage names are descriptive or evoke what Mount Desert meant to the early cottagers. "Fermata" is a musical notation meaning a pause or stop. Harold L. Randolph, the owner who named this cottage, was with the Boston Symphony.

32   Interview with Curtis Blake, July 2002. The family connection is plausible, but a Furness attribution must overcome the fact that all the surviving drawings are by Savage, and most importantly, the Tudor revival use of stucco, the Dutch door, and other details were characteristic of Savage's work at the time.

33   *Map of Harborside, Northeast Harbor, Maine, 1890, Fred L. Savage, architect.* Map 5449, Northeast Harbor Library. I am grateful to Robert R. Pyle for bringing this plat to my attention.

34   James T. Gardner, Director, *Report of New York State Survey for the year 1879, Part I, Special Report on the Preservation of Niagara Falls.* Courtesy of the National Park Service, Frederick Law Olmsted National Historic Site, Olmsted Records and Reports Collection, Brookline, Massachusetts. The spelling of Gardner's name varies; the "i" appears to be a twentieth-century addition.

35   James Grant Wilson and John Fiske, eds., *Appleton's Cyclopedia of American Biography* vol. II (New York: D. Appleton, 1898), 595; Laura Wood Roper, *FLO, A Biography of Frederick Law Olmsted* (Baltimore: The Johns Hopkins University Press, 1973), 282–283, 380, 395, 397.

36   Ray Palmer Baker, "James Terry Gardiner," *Dictionary of American Biography.* Reproduced in *Biography Resource Center* (Farmington Hills, Michigan: The Gale Group, 2003), http://www.galenet.com/servlet/biorc.

37   Gardner, *Report of New York State Survey*, 23.

38   Architectural Catalog, Northeast Harbor Library, 89, 8, 295-1.

39   An Old Summer Resident [W. W. Vaughan], *Northeast Harbor Reminiscences* (n.p.: White & Horne, 1930), 62.

40   Fabian Franklin, *The Life of Daniel Coit Gilman* (New York: Dodd, Mead and Company, 1910), 416. See also letter from Herman L. Savage to Daniel C. Gilman, et al., October 19, 1891, *Hancock County Deeds*, Ellsworth, Maine, Book 256, page 329.

41   Herman L. Savage, Prop., *The Rock End* (Bar Harbor: Bar Harbor Record Print, 1895), n.p.

42   As quoted in Anon., *Early Aspects of Mt. Desert* (Seal-Harbor, Me.: W. M. Griswold, 1896), n.p.

43   Mrs. Lincoln Cromwell, "A Glimpse of Northeast Harbor in the Nineties" (July 31, 1950), typescript of a paper presented to the Cranberry Club, Northeast Harbor Library.

44   Reynolds, "My Recollections of Grandfather," 5.

45   *Scientific American Building Monthly* (December 1904), 120–121, 129.

46   Ibid.

47   Earle G. Shettleworth, Jr., *The Summer Cottages of Islesboro, 1890–1930* (Islesboro, Maine: Islesboro Historical Society, 1989), 10–19.

48   Ibid., 116–117.

49   Contractors active during the building boom on Islesboro included Charles B. Brown and Otto Nelson from Bangor, W. E. Schwartz of Camden and G. H. Wilbur of Dover-Foxcroft, W. H. Glover of Rockland, D. J. Manchester of Northeast Harbor. Shettleworth, *The Summer Cottages of Islesboro*, 120–124.

50   Photocopy from the files of the Maine Historic Preservation Commission. I am grateful to Earle G. Shettleworth, Jr., for access to these files.

51   Quoted by Shettleworth, *The Summer Cottages of Islesboro*, 113.

52   Maria G. van Rensselaer, "American Country Dwellings," *The Century Magazine*, vol. XXXII (June 1886): 209–210, quoted by Reed, *A Delight to All Who Know It*, 17.

53   *The Belfast Republican Journal*, November 28, 1895, as quoted by Shettleworth, *The Summer Cottages of Islesboro*, 87.

54   *Bangor Industrial Journal*, December 6, 1895, from the files of the Maine Historic Preservation Commission.

55   *Bangor Industrial Journal*, October 28, 1898.

Chapter III

1   For a discussion of the evolution of the shingle style see Roth, *Shingle Styles, Innovation and Tradition*, 35–39; see also Scully, *The Shingle Style and the Stick Style*, 130–154.

2   *U.S. Manuscript Census, 1900*, vol. T623, reel 592, Enumeration District no. 53, sheet no. 12. Alice Preble is listed as being single and having been born in May 1879.

3   *Bar Harbor Record*, August 23, 1899. The dimensions may have been altered as planning progressed, for the *Bangor Industrial Journal* reported on November 11, 1899, that the building was 112 by 45 feet with a piazza 16 feet deep "overlooking the golf links."

4   For illustrations see Scully, *The Architecture of Summer*, plate 27, the Short Hills Casino (1882–1883) by McKim, Mead and White; plate 29, the Washington Park Club (1883) by S. S. Beman; plate 82, the New York Athletic Club's Country Clubhouse (1888) by George Martin Huss; plate 88, the Summer Headquarters of the Portland Club (1888) by John Calvin Stevens; plate 122, the Lake St. Clair Fishing and Shooting Club (1890) by Rogers and MacFarlane; plate 151, the Burlingame Country Club Stable (1894) by A. Page Brown; and plate 180, the Nassau Country Club by Woodruff Leeming.

5   *Bar Harbor Record*, May 23, 1900.

6   Nelson W. Aldrich, Jr., *Old Money, The Mythology of America's Upper Class* (New York: Alfred A. Knopf, 1988), 49–53; see also Hale, *The Story of Bar Harbor*, 173.

7   Savage's participation in the Kebo Valley Club is an accepted local tradition. Among his drawings at the Northeast Harbor Library is a carefully drawn interior plan for the *Sabiarita*, a double-ended, sixty-five-foot twin-engine yatch. I have been unable to locate any records that would make this drawing meaningful.

8   R. H. Moon was Savage's foreman for many years. He directed construction on the J. L. Ketterlinus, the Edgar Scott, the W. J. Schieffelin, the J. C. Livingston, and the A. J. Cassatt cottages. He established himself in Bar Harbor in 1900 and "had charge of several of the largest crews ever employed in the building trade in Bar Harbor." *Bar Harbor Record*, June 27, 1906.

9   *Bar Harbor Record*, April 4, 1900. See Appendix II for other documents related to this controversy.

10   See Appendix II for a contemporary description of Savage's addition at Faraway.

11   *Bar Harbor Record*, September 19, 1900.

12   *Bangor Industrial Journal*, November 30, 1900.

13   A. C. Savage, a manuscript account book entitled "Account with A. C. & Geo A. Savage," in the collection of Rick Savage. At the head of the first page, A. C. Savage entered money spent prior to October 30, 1900, and among the first six entries is "F. L. Savage Bill $2,647.62." And in April 1902, A. C. "Paid F. L. Savage com. on Hotel $153.39." The initial payment must have been for plans and perhaps included repayments for materials ordered by Fred.

14   Edward N. Akin, *Flagler: Rockefeller Partner and Florida Baron* (The Kent State University Press: Kent, Ohio, 1988), 120–123; see also Hap Hatton, *Tropical Splendor: An Architectural History of Florida* (New York: Alfred A. Knopf, 1987), 22–25.

15   *The Bar Harbor Record*, February 6, 1901. Local historians differ about the proper spelling of the name of this cottage, but the *Bar Harbor Times*, July 25, 1914, notes that Mr. and Mrs. John Callendar Livingston were at Callendar House. Transcribed by Jared Knowles, "An Exploration of the Colonial Revival Through Selected Works of Fred Savage, Architect" (MA Thesis, Savannah College of Art and Design, 1994), 54–57.

16   Ibid.

17   Surviving catalogues from Savage's office include: *The Phoenix Wire Works, Catalogue No. 35*, Detroit, Mich., April 15, 1909; *Southern Beauty Enameled Ware*, the Cahill Iron Works, Chattanooga, Tenn., n.d.; *General Compressed Air House Cleaning Co.*, St. Louis, Mo., 1907; *Lignine Carvings, Ornamental Products Co.* Detroit, Mich., n.d.; *Hot Air Pumping Machines*, Rider-Ericsson Engine Co., Walden, N.Y., 1904; *Architectural Varnishes and Stains for Natural Woods, Murphy Varnish Co.*, Newark, Boston; Cleveland, St. Louis, Chicago, n.d.; *Modern House Cleaning Tools and Equipment Catalogue*, Vacuum House Cleaning Company, Saint Louis, Mo., n.d.; *Modern Lavatories*, Western Metal Supply Co., San Diego, Cal., n.d.; *Specifications and Instructions for Finishing New Woodwork and Floors*, S. C. Johnson & Son, Racine, Wis., n.d.; *The House of Silence, Linofelt Keeps out Noise, Heat, Cold*, Union Fibre Company, Winona, Minn., 1907.

18   *The Bar Harbor Record*, April 17, 1901.

19   Jeffery Karl Ochsner and Thomas C. Hubka, "H. H. Richardson: The Design of the William Watts Sherman House," *Journal of the Society of Architectural Historians* vol. 51, no. 2 (June 1992): 122, 136.

20 Many relevant illustrations from this journal are reproduced in Scully's *Architecture of the American Summer*; see pages 56–57, 72–73, 98, 104–105, 154, and 169.

21 Breakwater has been renamed and is now called Atlantique.

22 Elizabeth Mitchell Walter, "Jay Hambidge and the Development of the Theory of Dynamic Symmetry, 1902–1920" (Ph.D. diss., University of Georgia, 1978).

23 Raymond Strout, preeminent collector of Mount Desert ephemera, brought the Bear Brook Quarry invoice to my attention. An undated memorandum by George B. Dorr entitled "Bear Brook Quarry" states: "I opened Bear Brook Quarry some forty years ago to supply stone for the building of the Pulitzer tower. . . . Two houses built of it at that time . . . the Edgar Scott house . . . and the John Innes Kane house. . . . Fred L. Savage, an excellent local architect, was in charge of the work on these houses, the plans prepared by leading architects in Boston and New York [*sic*]. . . . Mr. Savage did the work so well that I place[d] the quarry thereafter in his hands to operate, which he continued to do till he died." Sawtelle Archive, Acadia National Park, Mount Desert, B3.F6.36, ANPA. I am grateful to Ronald Epp for bringing this document to my attention.

24 *Bar Harbor Record*, December 19, 1900; see Appendix II for a contemporary description of Savage's colonial revival interior.

25 *Bar Harbor Record*, December 19, 1900.

26 *Bar Harbor Record*, April 1, 1903.

27 *Scientific American Building Monthly*, March 1904, 56–7.

28 *Bar Harbor Record*, January 22, 1902.

29 Anne Archbold also held a fishing world's record, landing a sixty-pound wahoo on a twenty-five-pound test line in the Bahamas. *New York Times*, March 28, 1968.

30 *Bar Harbor Record*, March 30, 1904.

31 Ibid.

32 For notice of Savage's vacations, see the *Bar Harbor Record*, October 26, 1904, November 15, 1905; March 7, 1906; and April 14, 1917. For the trip to Florida in 1913, see typed extracts from the diary of Emily Manchester Savage (1834–1914), Fred's mother, in the collection of the Northeast Harbor library.

33 Charles W. Eliot, *The Right Development of Mount Desert* (privately printed, 1904). Beneath his name at the conclusion of the fourteen-page pamphlet, Eliot placed the date—December 25, 1903. He apparently meant for his readers to understand that the essay was intended as a gift to the island he loved.

34 According to President Eliot the idea for the Hancock County Trustees of Public Reservations was based on the work of his son, Charles Eliot, landscape architect, who had instigated the creation of the Massachusetts Board of Trustees of Public Reservations. See George B. Dorr, *Acadia National Park, Its Origin and Background* (Bangor: Burr Printing Company, 1942), 51–52.

35 Ibid., 7.

36 Ibid., 19–20.

37 *Bar Harbor Times*, July 25, 1914; August 15, 1914; and September 5, 1914.

38 Roger G. Reed, "Bar Harbor Cottages," 15–26.

39 The library was dedicated on August 29, 1907, and cost $2,520.38. Mary Lou Hodge, letter to the author, February 28, 2003.

40 E. R. Robson, *School Architecture. Being Practical Remarks on the Planning, Designing, Building, and Furnishing of School-Houses* (1874; reprint, New York: Humanities Press, 1972).

41 Quoted by Malcolm Seaborne in an introductory essay to the reprinted *School Architecture*, 22.

42 Robson, *School Architecture*, 74.

43 Ibid., 178.

44 Ibid., 265–266.

45 For a description of the Washington Normal School in Machias see the *Bangor Industrial Journal*, December 1909, April 1910, June 1910, and August 1910.

46 Fred L. Savage to C. H. Burt, April 16, 1908; and Fred L. Savage to Morris McDonnald, February 10, 1916, typescript letters in the collection of the Mount Desert Historical Society, Town of Mount Desert.

47 Attributed to Fred L. Savage, "Beautiful Bar Harbor," 8. A seventeen-page typescript in the collection of the Mount Desert Historical Society. The complete text is reproduced in the Appendix.

48   Hale, Jr., *The Story of Bar Harbor*, 208–209. See also Helfrich and O'Neil, *Lost Bar Harbor*, 110.

49   Savage, "Beautiful Bar Harbor," 9.

50   For a history of the movement see William H. Wilson, *The City Beautiful Movement* (Baltimore: The Johns Hopkins University Press, 1989). See also John W. Reps, *The Making of Urban America* (Princeton: Princeton University Press, 1965), 497–525.

51   *Bar Harbor Times*, March 22 and 29, 1919. Although they both worked on Mount Desert, Farrand and Savage never worked on the same site at the same time. At different times, they both worked at the cottages Haven in Northeast Harbor and Chilton and Buonriposa in Bar Harbor. See Diana Balmori, Diane Kostial McGuire, and Eleanor M. McPeck, *Beatrix Farrand's American Landscapes, Her Gardens and Campuses* (Sagaponack, N.Y.: Sagapress, 1985).

52   Gary Stellpflug, "Ironwork," *Friends of Acadia Journal* (Summer/Fall 2000): 11–12. See also Acadia National Park Official Website, "Paths into the Past," *www.nps.gov/acad/trails.htm*.

53   *Bar Harbor Record*, August 16, 1905. The poll was conducted by the Bar Harbor Village Improvement Association, and the vote against cars was 105 to 0. Arthur Train published a satirical essay about the potential impact of automobiles. He predicted aggressive drivers, cars clustered at scenic spots, an "invasion" of transients who would contribute little to the economy and whose pervasive presence would drive cottagers away. He titled his essay "A Prophecy, the Isle of Mt. Deserted"; see *Bar Harbor Record*, August 28, 1907.

54   *Bar Harbor Record*, August 16, 1905.

55   *Bar Harbor Record*, December 9, 1908.

56   *Bar Harbor Times*, August 29, 1914.

57   The Franklin was made by the H. H. Franklin Manufacturing Company, 1901–1917, and subsequently by the Franklin Automobile Co., 1917–1934, both based in Syracuse, New York. They sold thirteen cars in 1902; sales rose to 13,000 during the 1925–1926 model year. An early four-cylinder Franklin cost $1,800; an early six-cylinder Franklin cost $4,000. By the late 1920s, a large Franklin with all the options could cost as much as $7,200.

58   *Bar Harbor Record*, April 9, 1913.

59   *Bar Harbor Times*, September 26, 1914.

60   *Bar Harbor Times*, February 13, 1915.

61   Although Savage prepared plans for the Islesford Hotel, the project was never built. Robert R. Pyle, conversation with the author, April 2003.

62   Reed, *A Delight to All Who Know It*, 134.

63   Josephine Morrison, "Notes on the Photographs," a manuscript accompanying the album, *Hauterive, 1899*, in the collection of the Bar Harbor Historical Society.

64   *Bar Harbor Record*, October 13, 1915.

65   Morrison, "Notes on the Photographs."

66   Ibid.

67   The total value of the real estate was $18,900, with the total estate value at $24,691.62.

68   *Probate Court Docket & Index to Records, 1923 to* [n.d.], *Hancock County* [Maine], vol. 4, page 64, case no. 10825, Estate of Fred L. Savage, Bar Harbor. The will was filed March 11, 1924, vol. 172, page 363; the amended account was filed and settled July 20, 1926, vol. 213, page 97.

69   Robert Pyle, conversation with the author, June 2004.

Appendix

1   Carbon copy, Mount Desert Island Historical Society.

2   Carbon copy, Mount Desert Island Historical Society.

3   Typescript among Savage's papers, Mount Desert Historical Society. Internal evidence suggests that it was written in 1915.

Upper Hadlock Pond,
Acadia National Park

Appendix

A Preliminary List of Buildings and Projects by Savage

This working list of buildings and projects by Savage is not complete, since the drawings, most of which are still rolled as they were in Savage's office and must be handled gingerly, are not yet fully catalogued and conserved. The list is based on drawings in the Northeast Harbor Library and the Mount Desert Island Historical Society, on the architectural surveys by T. Mark Cole, and the newspaper survey by Roger G. Reed, as well as unpublished sources cited above in the text.

I hope this preliminary list, which presents a sketch of Savage's career, will prompt others to add the details needed to develop a more sharply focused, full-blown portrait. Readers who wish to register corrections or additions to this list are urged to contact either the Northeast Harbor Library or the Mount Desert Island Historical Society. As nearly as possible, Savage's commissions are listed in chronological order. The traditional cottage name, if any, the client, location, dates, and commission numbers (where available) are given; buildings that are not securely dated appear at the end of each section of the list. Unless noted otherwise, Savage should be considered the design architect.

Residential Commissions

The Wedge for Herman L. Savage, Northeast Harbor, 1885–1887

Rockend Colonial, also known as the Yellow House, for Herman L. Savage, Northeast Harbor, 1885–1887

Ye Haven, attributed to John D. Clark; additions and alterations by J. Frederick Kelly, architect; Fred L. Savage, supervising architect; for James T. Gardiner, Northeast Harbor, after 1885

Random Ridge for Joseph P. Curtis, Northeast Harbor, 1885–1890

Northerly/Westerly for Lt. R. G. Davenport, Northeast Harbor, 1886–1887

Faraway for Mrs. John Harrison, Bar Harbor, 1886

Over Cliff, additions for H. R. Baltz and J. Hopkinson, location unknown, 1886–1887

Grasslands for Samuel D. Sargent, Northeast Harbor, 1886–1888

Watersmeet, also known as Point d'Acadie, additions and alterations for George Vanderbilt, Bar Harbor, 1887

Hilltop for Mr. and Mrs. Fred L. Savage, Northeast Harbor, 1887

K. J. Stevens Cottage, Northeast Harbor, 1887

A. C. Wheelwright Cottage, Northeast Harbor, 1888

Morris Cottage for Dr. Caspar Morris, Northeast Harbor, 1888–1889

Havenwood, also known as Mainstream, for J. D. Phillips, Northeast Harbor, 1889

Phillips Cottage for Frederick I. Phillips, Northeast Harbor, 1889–1890

L'Escale for Benjamin W. Arnold, Northeast Harbor, 1890

Fermata for Harold Randolph, Northeast Harbor, 1890

Aerie for Helen B. Howe,
Northeast Harbor, 1890

Isis for Dr. John C. Jay and Mrs. Peter Jay,
Northeast Harbor, 1890

Grey Pine for Agnes and Sophie Irwin,
Northeast Harbor, 1890

Sweet Briar for Anna Davis,
Northeast Harbor, 1890

Wagstaff for Miss Robert,
Northeast Harbor, 1890

Journey's End for Dr. and Mrs. Joseph Tunis,
Commission #073, Northeast Harbor, 1890

Hillbrook for Mrs. Hunter,
Northeast Harbor, 1890

Hard-a-Lee for Mrs. W. C. Doane,
Northeast Harbor, 1890

Ready About for Mrs. W. C. Doane,
Northeast Harbor, 1890

Rosserne for Rev. Cornelius B. Smith,
Northeast Harbor, 1891

Ogston Cottage, also known as Hillside, for
Mrs. R. Ogston, Northeast Harbor, 1891

Stone Ledge for Clara Williamson,
Northeast Harbor, 1892–1897

Birchcroft for Carrol S. Tyson,
Northeast Harbor, 1892

Hillcrest, Stratton & Quimby, architects, 1887;
addition for Rueben Hoyt by Savage,
Bar Harbor, 1892

The Ledge for W. W. Vaughn,
Northeast Harbor, 1892

Reverie Cove for Mrs. John Jones,
Bar Harbor, 1892

The Anchorage, Rotch & Tilden, architects,
1885; additions and alterations by Savage for
Miss E. H. Elwood, Bar Harbor, 1893

Ellwood, also known as the Anchorage, additions
and alterations for Mrs. E. S. Randoph Cottage,
Bar Harbor, 1893

Brackenfell for Professor C. K. Adams, Savage
and Stratton, architects, Northeast Harbor,
1893–1897

Warren P. Lombard Cottage, Savage and
Stratton, architects, location unknown, 1894

Old Farm, Henry Richards, architect (1894);
alterations and outbuildings by Savage for
George B. Dorr, location unkown, 1900, 1904

Ella Williamson Cottage, Savage and Stratton,
architects, Islesboro, 1894–1895

Journey's End for Mrs. Caspar Wister, Northeast
Harbor, 1895

The Steep Ways Stable for Dr. William T.
Helmuth, Bar Harbor, 1895

Eastward Way for Clarence Kimball,
Northeast Harbor, 1895

Ketterlinus Cottage, architect unknown; Savage
and Stratton, supervising architects,
Bar Harbor, 1895

Ledgelawn for Frances Clark,
Northeast Harbor, 1895–1897

Mainstay, also known as Greencourt, Rotch &
Tilden, architects, 1883; alterations for Charlotte
Pendleton by Savage, Bar Harbor, 1895

Inch Cape for Dr. William R. Huntington,
Northeast Harbor, 1895

Overedge for Daniel Coit Gilman,
Northeast Harbor, 1895

Semi-detached Cottages for Mrs. A. C. Savage,
Colorado Springs, Colorado, 1895

George Philler Cottage, Savage and Stratton,
architects, Islesboro, 1895–1896

Mizzentop, J. Pickering Putnam, architect, 1884;
alterations for B. Hall McCormick by Savage,
Bar Harbor, 1895

Paul B. Valle Cottage, Savage and Stratton, architects, Islesboro, 1896

Bide-a-While for J. L. Ketterlinus, Frank Miles
Day, architect; Savage and Stratton, supervising
architects, Bar Harbor, 1896

Ravensthorp for James G. Thorp, Savage and
Stratton, architects, Greenings Island, 1896

Over-the-Way, also known as the Alders, for
Samuel D. Sargent, Northeast Harbor, 1896

The Parsonage for Rev. A. S. H. Windsor, Savage
and Stratton, architects, Seal
Harbor, 1896

Miss F. A. L. Haven Cottage, Savage and
Stratton, architects, Jaffery,
New Hampshire, 1897.

W. W. Vaughn Cottage, Seal Harbor, 1897

Sweet Pea, architect unknown, 1887; additions for
James E. Foster by Savage and Stratton,
Bar Harbor, 1897

Hilltop, also known as the Eliot Cottage, for Dr.
Samuel A. Eliot, Savage and Stratton, architects,
Northeast Harbor, 1897

Harbor Cottage, addition and alterations for A.
C. Savage, Savage and Stratton, architects,
Northeast Harbor, 1898

Bragdon Cottage for Sara Bragdon,
Northeast Harbor, 1898

Col. Edward Morrell Cottage, also known as
Thirlstane, addition by Cope and Stewardson,
architects; Savage and Stratton, supervising
architects, Bar Harbor, 1898

Charles Plant Cottage, Savage and Stratton,
architects, Bar Harbor, 1898

Rev. William Prall Cottage, Savage and
Stratton, architects, Islesboro, 1897–1898

Strawberry Hill, Rotch & Tilden, architects,
1888; additions for J. Frederick May by Savage
and Stratton, Bar Harbor, 1898

Foresight, addition for Miss Davidson, Savage
and Stratton architects, Northeast Harbor,
1898

The Moorings, Burnham & Root, architects,
1885; addition for H. D. Gibson by Savage
and Stratton, Bar Harbor, 1898

Mrs. John W. Minturn Cottage,
Islesboro, 1898–1899

George S. Silsbee Cottage,
Islesboro, 1898–1899

Charles Platt, Sr., Cottage, 1898–1899, addition 1900, commission #109, Islesboro

Wadsworth-Larson Cottage for Giedion Scull,
commission #100, Northeast Harbor, 1899

Lucy Howe and Arthur Brooks Cottage,
Northeast Harbor, 1899

Dr. William H. Draper Cottage,
Islesboro, 1899

J. M. Whitmore Cottage, commission #126,
Northeast Harbor, 1899, 1901

Herman A. Lewis Cottage, Islesboro, Cope
and Stewardson, architects; Fred L. Savage,
supervising architect, Islesboro, 1899

Harbor Cottage, alterations and additions for
A. C. Savage, Northeast Harbor, 1900

Hillcrest, Stratton & Quimby, architects, 1887;
addition for Thomas Hubbard (or Mrs. Hoyt)
by Savage, Bar Harbor, 1900

Stornaway, Wheelwright & Haven, architects,
1884; additions by Savage for Moorfield
Storey, Northeast Harbor, 1900

Faraway, Furness, Evans & Co., architects,
1885; additions for Mrs. John Harrison by
Savage, Bar Harbor, 1900

Callendar House for John C. Livingston,
Bar Harbor, 1900

279

Wildacre for George S. Robbins,
Bar Harbor, 1900–1901

Beau Desert, William Ralph Emerson, architect,
1881; renovations for Augustus C. Gurnee by
Savage, Bar Harbor, 1900

West View for Ansel Manchester,
Northeast Harbor, 1900

Nearwoods, also known as Gruvie, for Ansel
Manchester, Northeast Harbor, 1900

Sunset Ledge for George W. Pepper, commission
#113, Northeast Harbor, 1900

Skyview, also known as the Mrs. Lawrence
Lewis Cottage, commission #114,
Northeast Harbor, 1900

Reef Point for W. B. Frazier, commission #117,
Northeast Harbor, 1900

J. C. Havemeyer Cottage, commission #118,
Seal Harbor, 1900

Fiddler's Green for George Savage,
Northeast Harbor, 1900

Treetops for Rev. William Adams Brown,
Seal Harbor, 1900

Bird Bank for A. C. Savage,
Northeast Harbor, 1900

Richard Heckscher Cottage, Newman Woodman
and Harris, architects; Fred L. Savage supervising architect, Northeast Harbor, 1900

Charles Platt, Jr., Cottage, Islesboro, 1900

Birds Nest for John Savage,
Northeast Harbor, 1900–1902

Devilstone, Rotch & Tilden, architects, 1885;
addition for Clement B. Newbold by Savage,
Bar Harbor, 1901

Mary H. Williams Cottage, commission #124,
Northeast Harbor, 1901

No View, also known as the Ralph Cottage for I.
E. Ralph, commission #127,
Northeast Harbor, 1901

Colonial Cottage, also known as Torworth, for
Bradford Fraley, Northeast Harbor, 1901.

Sunnie Holme for John Falt, commission #134,
Northeast Harbor, 1901

Carriage House for Andrew C. Wheelwright,
Northeast Harbor, 1901

Candage Cottage for C.A. Candage,
Northeast Harbor, 1901

Strawberry Hill, Rotch & Tilden, architects,
1888; addition by Savage for J. Frederick May,
Bar Harbor, 1901

Tullibardine for Miss M. H. Guthrie,
Bar Harbor, 1901

Weld Cottage, architect unknown, 1869; addition
by Savage for C. M. Weld, Bar Harbor, 1901

Whileaway, also known as the Mrs. John
Trevor Cottage, for George Vanderbilt,
Bar Harbor, 1901

Vista Cottage for Fred L. Savage,
Bar Harbor, 1902

Cedar Cliff, also known as Hill Crest, for George
L. Stebbins; Andres, Jacques and Rantoul, archi-
tects; Savage and Stratton, supervising architects,
Seal Harbor, 1902

The Ledges for G. Mary Williams,
Northeast Harbor, 1902

Atlantean for Fred L. Savage, Bar Harbor, 1903

Hillcrest for George Stebbins, Seal Harbor, 1902

Schiefflin Cottage, A.W. Longfellow, architect;
Fred L. Savage, supervising architect,
Bar Harbor, 1902

Dr. Alexander W. Biddle Cottage,
Islesboro, 1902–1903

Harbor Villa for Merritt Ober, commission #275,
Northeast Harbor, 1903

Archbold Cottage, architect unknown; Fred L.
Savage, supervising architect, Bar Harbor, 1903

Breakwater, also known as Atlantique, for John I.
Kane, Bar Harbor, 1903

S. W. Bridgeham Cottage, Bar Harbor, 1903

Ardeen for Mrs. Carol Mercer [?],
Bar Harbor, c. 1903

Alice M. Clark Cottage, Northeast Harbor, 1904

George W. Guthrie Cottage, alterations,
Bar Harbor, 1904

Aldersea, George W. Orff, architect, 1874; additions for Edward and Mary R. Coles by Savage,
Bar Harbor, 1904

Buena Vista, architect unknown, 1881; alterations for Dr. J. T. Hinch, Bar Harbor, 1904

Sunset Shore for Miss E. P. Sohier,
Northeast Harbor, 1904

Ledgelawn Inn for S. W. Bridgham,
Bar Harbor, 1904

Amberside for Frank T. Howard,
Hulls Cove, 1906

Firwood for E. V. Douglas, Seal Harbor, 1907

John Crosby Brown Cottage, commission #234,
Seal Harbor, 1907

Juniper Ledge for George Walton Green (or
Greene), Northeast Harbor, 1907–1909

Royeden for David James King,
Bar Harbor, c. 1910

Reading Room (cabin) for Rev. William Adams
Brown, commission #263, Seal Harbor, 1910

Grey Rock for William S. Grant, commission
#268, Northeast Harbor, 1911

Sound Edge for Rev. Reese F. Alsop, Albert E.
Parfitt, architect; Fred L. Savage, supervising
architect, Northeast Harbor, 1911

Wyandotte, J. E. Clark, architect, 1884;
alterations for Mr. Parker by Savage,
Bar Harbor, 1911

Mrs. Biddle Porter Cottage, Bar Harbor, 1911

High Seas for Prof. Rudolph E. Brunnow,
Bar Harbor, 1911

Rev. William Prall–Harold I. Pratt Cottage, additions and alterations, Islesboro, 1911–1912.

Mark Morrison House, alterations,
Bar Harbor, 1912

H. O. Schirmer Cottage, Bar Harbor, 1912

Chiltern, 1895, William Longfellow, architect;
Fred L. Savage, supervising architect; alterations
for Edgar T. and Maisie Sturgis Scott by Savage,
Bar Harbor, 1900

Hauterive, also known as Edenfield, William
Ralph Emerson, architect, 1881; additions and
alterations by Savage for Mrs. Miles B.
Carpenter, Bar Harbor, 1915

A. Veazie-Kedge Cottage, architect unknown,
1871; alterations for Mrs. William Sterling by
Savage, Bar Harbor, 1916

Tanglewold, attributed to William Ralph
Emerson, architect; alterations for Murray Young
by Savage, Bar Harbor, 1917

Buonriposo, Grosvenor Atterbury, architect,
1904; rebuilt to Ernesto G. Fabbri's design;
Fred L. Savage supervising architect,
location unknown, 1919

Hauterive, also known as Edenfield, William
Ralph Emerson, architect, 1881; alterations of
stable by Savage for Mrs. Miles B. Carpenter,
Bar Harbor, 1921.

Thrush Woods for William Jay Turner,
Northeast Harbor, 1921

Hauterive Garage for Agnes Carpenter,
Bar Harbor, 1921–1924

Immensee for Samuel S. Fels, Seal Harbor, 1922

Tanglewood Cottage, Northeast Harbor, 1923

Undated Residential Commissions

Baptist Parsonage, Northeast Harbor

A. W. Bunker Cottage, Bar Harbor

Miss Nellie Butler Cottage, Northeast Harbor

A. J. Cassett Gate Lodge and Stable, Bar Harbor

E. W. Clark Cottage, alterations, location unknown

Miss Francis Clark Cottage, Northeast Harbor

Alice M. Clarke Cottage, commission #134, location unknown

Alfred M. Coats Stable, Bar Harbor

Alfred M. Coats Cottage, additions by Clarke and Howe, architects; Fred L. Savage, supervising architect, Bar Harbor

Charles M. Conners Cottage, Bar Harbor

Cooksey Stable, Bar Harbor

Edwin P. Corning Camps, Northeast Harbor

Alexander Mosely Davis Cottage, Northeast Harbor

Mary Pearl Evans Cramp Cottage, Redlands, California

Jim Foster Cottage, Bar Harbor

Cove Cottage for Abram Gilpatrick, Northeast Harbor

Hastings Cottage, Somesville

S. D. Hecht Cottage, Bar Harbor

Henderson Cottage, Bar Harbor

Howard Hickle Hot House, Bar Harbor

Mrs. E. L. Homens Cottage, Bar Harbor

George Hopkins Cottage, Northeast Harbor

Frank T. Howard Cottage, Hulls Cove

Thomas H. Hubbard Cottage and Stable, Bar Harbor

Judge George L. Ingraham Cott Mantle, Bar Harbor

Charles C. Ladd Cottage, Bar Harbor

A. E. Lawrence Cottage, Bar Harbor

Arthur Little Cottage, Little and Browne, architects; Fred L. Savage supervising architect, Bar Harbor

I. F. C. Lyman Cottage, Bar Harbor

Sarah May Cottage, Bar Harbor

Myra E. Morrison Cottage, Bar Harbor

Moseley Hall additions, for Alexander Moseley, Savage and Stratton, architects, Bar Harbor,

Calvin H. Norris Cottage, Bar Harbor

Parker Cottage, Bar Harbor

Dr. J. J. Patten Cottage and Office, Bar Harbor

Charlotte Pendelton Cottage and Stable, Bar Harbor

Ardeen, for Agnes E. Platt, Bar Harbor

E. S. Randolph Cottage, additions and alterations, Bar Harbor

William B. Rice Cottage, Bar Harbor

Agamont Hotel cottages, for Tobias L. Roberts, Bar Harbor

George A. Savage Cottage, Northeast Harbor

Willow Cottage for Herman L. Savage, Northeast Harbor

Miss Sears Porch and Fence, West Gouldsboro

Mrs. William T. Sedwick Cottage, Savage and Stratton, architects, location unknown

Frank A. Sherman Stable, Bar Harbor

Schifflin Stable for George W. Vanderbilt, Bar Harbor

W. H. Shuman Cottage, Bar Harbor

Elmer and Helen Smallidge Mantels, Northeast Harbor

Sonogee Cottage, Bar Harbor

Evergreen Hedge for Mrs. J. K. Stevens, Northeast Harbor

Augustus Thorndike Pier, Bar Harbor

P. S. Thorsen House, North Hancock, Maine

Willis Towne Cottage, Seal Harbor

S. R. Tracey Cottage, alterations and additions, Northeast Harbor

Trevor Cottage and Stables, Bar Harbor

William R. Dupree Cottage, Peabody and Stearns, architects; Fred L. Savage supervising architect, location unknown

Mrs. Francis Patterson Cottage alterations, Northeast Harbor

Miss Zabriskie Cottage, Northeast Harbor

Commercial and Institutional Buildings

Harborside Inn for James Terry Gardiner and Frank (or William) Wiswell, Northeast Harbor, 1890

Northeast Harbor Reading Room for Daniel Coit Gilman et al., Northeast Harbor, 1891

Northeast Harbor Library, 1892

Milton Allen Store, Savage and Stratton, architects, Bar Harbor, 1895

Tobias L. Roberts Building, Savage and Stratton, architects, Bar Harbor, 1896

Architectural Office, Fred L. Savage, Bar Harbor, 1898

Dorr Building, Savage and Stratton, architects, Bar Harbor, 1898

Louisburg Hotel, addition, Bar Harbor, 1899

Pot and Kettle Club, Hulls Cove, 1899

Holly Hill for Frederick I. Phillips, commission #135, Northeast Harbor, 1899, 1901

Kebo Valley Club, Wilson Eyre, architect, 1888; redesigned by Savage, Bar Harbor, 1899

Asticou Inn for A. C. Savage, commission #121, Northeast Harbor, 1900

Gilman High School, commission #231, Northeast Harbor, 1906

West Gouldsboro Library, commission #232, West Gouldsboro, 1906

Northeast Harbor School, addition, Northeast Harbor, 1906

Bar Harbor High School, Bar Harbor, 1907

Sherman's Store, Bar Harbor, 1908

Washington County Normal School, commission #260, Machias, 1910

Jesup Library, Delano & Aldrich, architects; Fred L. Savage supervising architect, Bar Harbor, 1910

Fire Station, Bar Harbor, 1911

C. L. Morang Store, Bar Harbor, 1912

Islesboro Inn, additions, Evans Warner and
Register, architects, Fred L. Savage, supervising
architect, Islesboro, 1912

Pastime Theater for William Dolliver, commission #281, Northeast Harbor, 1913

Union Church, Peabody and Stearns,
architects, alterations by Fred L. Savage,
Northeast Harbor, 1913

Malvern Hotel annex, Bar Harbor, 1915

Otter Cliffs Radio Station, Bar Harbor, 1917

Movie Theater for D.H. Mayo, Southwest
Harbor, 1918

Jessup Library, renovation, Bar Harbor

M. Franklin Store, Bar Harbor

Bar Harbor Hospital, alterations, Bar Harbor

Electric Company, Bar Harbor

Bowling Alley, Bar Harbor

Comfort Station, Bar Harbor

Louisburg Hotel, Hamilton Cottage, Bar Harbor

Mount Block Company Building, also known
as Bar Harbor Bank and Trust Company,
Bar Harbor

Newport Hotel cottage, Bar Harbor

Grammar School (Heald Building), alterations,
Bar Harbor

Green Brothers Store, Bar Harbor

N. Hillson and Son Store, Bar Harbor

Neighborhood House, Seal Harbor

Hamor and Stanley Building Supply Store,
Northeast Harbor

Isolated Hospital, Bar Harbor

YWCA Building, alterations, Bar Harbor

Northeast Harbor Float

Rockend Hotel, alterations, Northeast Harbor

Rockend Hotel Pier, Northeast Harbor

Dr. J. D. Phillips Store, Northeast Harbor

Gilman High School, Northeast Harbor

Seal Harbor School, Seal Harbor

Seal Harbor Neighborhood House, Seal Harbor

William Ward Store, Manset, Maine

Projects

Electric Company, Bar Harbor, 1899

Dr. J. H. Patten Cottage and Office,
location unknown, 1910

Second Islesboro Inn, Islesboro, c. 1916

Mrs. W. Earl Dodge, Jr. Cottage, Islesboro, 1903

Andrew C. Wheelwright Cottage,
Northeast Harbor, c. 1901

Bangor High School, Bangor, Maine

R. H. Kittridge Cottage, Proposed Refrigeration,
location unknown

Spring Inn, Northeast Harbor

Mrs. E. B. Rodick, Camp at Eagle Lake, location
unknown

In His Own Words: Selected Writings by and attributed to Savage

[A letter concerning the Carpenter's Union and the Scott cottage controversy, published in the *Bar Harbor Record*, April 4, 1900]

Preliminary Correspondence. The following correspondence between Mr. Fred Savage, the contractor of the Scott job, and the carpenters union was received at the Record office too late for last week's issue:

Bar Harbor, Me. March 26, 1900

To Mr. John Burr and the Carpenters' Labor Union, Bar Harbor, Me.:

Gentlemen: The following is a statement of my position in regard to the discharging of the men at the Scott house.

In the first place, as you know, one of my men left the job assumedly because you made matters so unpleasant for him that he did not care to stay. This was the first word that came to my ears that there was a union, or that there was a single note of discord among us. I confess that I was very much annoyed, and vexed that there was an organized order aiming to make trouble and discontent on the job. Up to that time I had full confidence in my men, believing that you all had done your best and would go hand in hand with me through the work.

After this matter had been discussed between us I had an interview with your president, a man I have always held in high esteem, and was assured by him that no demands would be made on the job, and that no man should be pressed into the union against his will. This of course set me right at once, and I should have had no grievance today if this spirit had been carried out. But on the part of a few of the men in your union it has not; and their manner toward Mr. Moon, my foreman, and towards some of the other workmen on the job who have not wished to join the union, has not been as pleasant as it should have been, and therefore they were not doing their best for the interest of their employer. For this reason I decided to discharge all those who showed by their manner and idleness that they were not wholly satisfied and ready to do their best to give an honest equivalent in labor for the money they received.

There is a majority of men in your organization whom I would like to have back to work, and if they will report to Mr. Moon I will leave it entirely in his hands to hire them if he feels that he has full confidence in their ability and good faith to try and work for our interests, not to allow themselves to carry any hard feelings either against me or any one on the job, union or non union, and to see that the spirit of the promise to carry the job through without any trouble, is carried out by them. I appeal to you as honest men to stand by that promise; and those of you who did not receive their money at the job on

Saturday afternoon, (for the reason stated above) shall be used with all fairness and without prejudice or feeling of any kind.

I want it plainly understood that I have not discharged any man simply because he belonged to the union, if so, I should have served all alike, but, as above stated, because I felt that some were not working for the interests of the job. I have always exercised this privilege, and do not believe there is one among you who would wish to have it go on record that I should not do so in this case.

Please consider this matter carefully at your meeting tonight, and I believe you will know that it will be better for us both to work together as we should. Many of you have been given work on my houses for years, and I feel sure you do not wish to sever our friendly relations by any hasty act. I will be glad to see any of you at my office at any time you wish an interview. Leaving this matter entirely in your hand to act upon as seems best to you, I remain,

Yours very truly,
Fred L. Savage

[Additions to Faraway designed by Fred L. Savage, as described in the *Bar Harbor Record*, December 19, 1900; attributed to F. L. Savage]

The additions that are being made to Faraway cottage, the summer home of Mrs. John Harrison on Eagle Lake Road is virtually transforming the present structure into one of the large residences of the village. Last summer when Mrs. Harrison decided to enlarge her house she called to her assistance her architect, Mr. Fred L. Savage, and laid the case before him. How admirably has Mr. Savage succeeded in the plans he submitted the guests of Mrs. Harrison have ample opportunity to verify. The extension is on the western side of the house on the line of Eagle Lake Road and is nearly 70 feet in length and 28 feet in width. It is two story in height, surmounted with a gambrel roof ornamented with dormer windows.

The first story is clapboard and all the rest of the house is finished in shingles. In adjusting the new addition to the older house the roof of the latter had to be considerably enlarged so that in the imposing front that is now presented the former house will hardly be recognized.

And the new house has a feature, and a striking feature too. It is the dining room. The brief description we can give will do scant justice to the thought of the architect who planned it or the ability of the contractor, A. E. Lawrence, who is carrying out that thought.

In size the dining room is 17 by 28 feet. In finish the details are purely colonial and are very elaborate. Fluted ionic columns topped with carved capitals and elliptic arches, adorn the walls. A handsome wainscoting extends around the room, the walls of which are finished in panels. On one side of the room is a large open fireplace and a mantel designed in strict details of the other finish. An elaborate frieze of scroll work extends the full width of the mantel. Surmounting the shelf is a plate glass mirror set in a carved gilt frame.

On the north side of the dining room is a large bay window which opens out on the porch. On the south side of the room and separated from it by an elliptical arch is a pretty alcove, with foxed seating extending the full width, and a window which gives a good view of the road in front.

Separated from the dining room by sliding doors is the smoking room. And this too is an attractive feature. It is 15 to 17 feet in size with open fireplace. The room is finished in quartered oak and the mantel is of the same material. The handsome wainscoting and beamed ceiling are very effective. The smoking room contains a large bookcase and an old fashioned settle. An opening on the north side leads to the terrace which is connected with the wide porch. The terrace and porch extend nearly the entire length of the house on the north side.

To the left of the main entrance to the house is a hall extending the entire length of the new addition, separating a number of rooms from the dining room and smoking room. The first is the wine closet, the second is the butler's pantry, which is furnished with the latest improved devices, and is made more attractive by a neat bay window. Next is the toilet room and then the pantry. The extreme north-western portion of the new addition is occupied by the kitchen and servant's dining room.

The second floor is divided into five bedrooms and two bathrooms. Two of the bedrooms have open fireplaces and all the rooms have ample closets.

As we have already said the design for this new addition was furnished by Mr. Fred L. Savage, architect, whose success has so often been demonstrated that but little new can be said. . . . Of the builder and contractor, A. E. Lawrence, it can be said that he is faithfully carrying out Mr. Savage's idea, and that too, in an enthusiastic manner. In finish and workmanship is leaving nothing to be desired. Martin Lord is foreman of the carpenters, and is carefully attending to the details of his department.

The plumbing is being done by Leighton, Davenport and Co., the painting by Graham and Co. and the mason work by Shea and Preble, all of whom are sustaining their well earned reputation.

[A description of Reverie Cove, *Bar Harbor Record*, May 11, 1893; attributed to F. L. Savage]

On Prospect Avenue and facing the bay there is being erected a very pretty summer home for Mrs. John D. Jones of Washington D.C. While Mrs. Jones has spent several summers at Northeast Harbor, she has never been a cottager here, but so taken had she become with the beauty of Bar Harbor that last fall she purchased this lot and had the erection of a beautiful summer cottage commenced. The style of the house is that of an Italian villa and with its broad piazzas and massive proportion makes an extremely attractive building. It is to be treated in a plaster treatment in imitation of stone, the preparation being put on over the most improved iron lathe sheathing.

Entering from the broad piazza to a small vestibule some 10 by 10 in size, one passes from that into the big reception hall, which is 30 by 40 and finished in a very pleasing manner. From this is the grand stairway, in two parts, to the floor above, from whence the chambers are reached by a broad and airy hall. From this hall open six large chambers and a boudoir and four dressing rooms. There are two large bath rooms and all necessary toilet conveniences. Fireplaces are in many of the rooms on this floor and in addition registers furnish heat from large furnaces in the basement. On the third floor are the servants' apartments and they are finished neatly and with taste.

On the first floor and opening from the main reception room are the dining room, parlor and smoking room, all finished in a handsome manner.

The house has a basement story and in it are the kitchen, laundry, pantry and the men's room. Take it all in all the house will make a very pretty and desirable summer home.

Mr. F. L. Savage is the architect and contractor and the house was built under the supervision of his foreman, Mr. B. W. Candage. The grounds will be prettily laid out under the direction of the landscape gardener, Mr. Isaac N. Mitchel.

Bar Harbor Board of Trade[1]

April 16, 1908

Mr. C.M. Burt
Boston, Mass.

Dear Sir:

On behalf of the Bar Harbor Board of Trade I have been corresponding with Col. Boothby of the Maine Central on the subject of a series of excursions to Bar Harbor during the months of June and July from points on the route to Boston. The last letter I had from Col. Boothby on the subject, informed me that he had been to Boston and consulted with you in regard to the matter, and he gave me to understand that your roads did not care to give reduced rates after July first, and that, judging from past experience, you thought the cost of advertising an excursion for June would be about $400 of which naturally you would expect us to pay about three-fourths.

As Col. Boothby thought it might save confusion if I corresponded directly with you, I wish to inform you that after giving the matter careful consideration the Directors of the Board of Trade have come to the conclusion that it would be unwise to try to handle any kind of excursion this year as the funds for advertising purposes are already pretty well used up in the printing and distribution of a large edition of booklets advertising Bar Harbor, and also because our hotel men do not feel like making any reduction after the first of July, and the hotels that open previous to that date are very few and are not pre-pared to handle anything of a crowd, unless previously assured of it. These few hotels do not open until the latter part of June anyway.

Part of our working program for the ensuing year must be to endeavor to educate our people to the idea of trying to lengthen the season by making their hotels habitable during the months of May, June, and October, and thoroughly advertising that fact when it has been accomplished. Then we can afford to advertise excursions for which we will have no trouble in securing advantageous rates from all parties concerned.

I have written Mr. Boothby to this same effect, and have thanked him, as I wish cordially to thank you for the interest and trouble you have taken in this matter, and you may rest assured that anything we can do in return to help your Roads will be gladly done.

If you can handle any of our booklets to advantage, kindly let me know how many and I will have them forwarded to any addresses you may give me. The booklet is just large enough to go in a 6 3/4" envelope, contains twenty pages including cover with neat colored design, and is well illustrated with views of Bar Harbor. We shall have them from the printer in about a week.

Yours very truly,

Bar Harbor Board of Trade[2]

February 10, 1916

Mr. Morris McDonnald
Pres. Maine Central R. R.
Portland, Maine

My Dear Sir:
Pursuant to a request and on behalf of the Bar Harbor Board of Trade, I am writing to urge that you arrange your New York to Bar Harbor, through pullman service so that trains may begin somewhat earlier and continue later than in seasons past.

Indications point to a sharp increase in travel by tourists to Mt. Desert Island for the coming season and we believe that the hotels and cottages are going to be filled far in excess of normal capacity.

Many of the summer tourists express a wish to come earlier and stay later, but state that they are prevented from doing so on account of inadequate train service.

We believe the summer tourist business would be greatly enhanced and the season lengthened if the rail roads will extend this through pullman service for one month, beginning May 29th, and ending Oct. 14th, for this season, [instead of June 14th. To Oct. 3rd, as was the 1915 schedule.]

We believe the extension of this service for one month as above, will work to the mutual benefit of the rail roads as well as the community.

Will you kindly give this subject immediate consideration and let me have your reply in time to report before the Board of Trade at the next meeting which is called for next Wednesday evening.

Yours very truly,
(signed) Fred L Savage Ch. Comm.

[The draft of a promotional pamphlet, attributed to Fred L. Savage]

Beautiful Bar Harbor: Its Manifold Attractions[3]

"See Naples and die," was the advice of some old-world enthusiast. "See Bar Harbor and live," is our advice to those who can. Certainly the Bay of Naples has a worthy rival in Frenchman's Bay, which bathes the feet of beautiful Mount Desert, while the scenic charms, if different from those of the Italian coast, are equally alluring. And when it comes to invigorating, life-giving air, there is no comparison. To Bar Harbor men and women who are able to compare the beauty and joy of American's most delightful summer home with the health and happiness resorts of the whole globe return in throngs for rest and recreation. Their decision is unanimous. Bar Harbor gives them all that other places can and more besides. While one holiday resort is noted for its picturesque scenery, its lakes and mountains, another for its vivacity and social brilliancy, or for its unspoiled natural charm, and others yet for their bathing, yachting, golfing, or fishing facilities, or their admirable hotels, Bar Harbor combines them all. Do you want cheerful social intercourse: The place is full of it, with club and hotel life, with gaiety and music, with golf links, swimming pool, tea houses that one may motor to, and admirable roads for motoring. Do you prefer to be alone with the "sounding sea" for your companion, or to commune with nature face to face? Then stroll along the wonderful shore paths, with their ever-changing vistas of white-sailed yachts, blue sky and rocky islets, or climb the mountains by means of the well-tended pathways extending right across the island for scores of miles; drive or motor along the Ocean or Corniche roads, obtaining views which equal those of the world-famous French or Italian Riviera; or motor swiftly inland across the Bridge, and range at will up and down the most picturesque coast in America for forty or fifty miles.

Cost of Living
An idea yet prevails, sprung from a passing phase of its development, that Bar Harbor is a resort for the wealthy only. It is not true. As in its early days, so now, it yields as freely as nature does herself beauty and refreshment and manifold human interest to all who come to seek it. "Lordly pleasure houses" have been built along its shores undoubtedly, by men of wealth, but there are many others, and a great number, who know and love the Island, and who return to it year after year because not only is it beautiful and health-giving as well as socially attractive, but also because they find they can live there economically and in modest fashion. Hotels and opportunities for summer homes exist in abundance, suited

alike to every scale of means; and the great resources of the place, its beauty, and the climate given it by nature, the splendid spaciousness of the sea and mountains are alike free to all, as well as every public feature of its social life. And while it contains hotels of sumptuous luxury for those who seek them, there are others equally comfortable if less luxurious where visitors can enjoy themselves at moderate cost, yet find themselves among people accustomed to demand the best. Slightly to alter the words of Burns, "Wealth is not the guinea stamp" at Bar Harbor, nor does it open doors which would else be closed. On the contrary, for those who enjoy pleasant and cultured social intercourse without excessive emulation in the matter of expenditure it is an ideal spot.

Water Supply and Sanitation

Pure air alone does not fill the need of a great health resort. Pure water and first-class sanitation, that is, a modern and efficient drainage system, are essential to it also. Bar Harbor has these and more. Its atmosphere has a wonderfully invigorating quality—dry in spite of the sea's close neighborhood to temper its sunshine and the summer heat. The Island is clothed with northern evergreens whose resinous fragrance is noticed even far to sea. The water supply is incomparable, coming from a natural reservoir in the mountains a few miles from the town, whose whole watershed is now protected by being placed in public reservation. To drink this water or to wash in it is equally a delight, and it is piped to every house. Admirable too is the drainage system of the town, which ensures it against any chance of serious epidemic; while the milk and every other food supply is guarded by an efficient Board of Health appointed by the town, and by a Summer Resident and Physicians' Committee, of which Dr. Robert Abbe, of New York, famous surgeon and devoted summer resident of Bar Harbor—is the head.

Motoring

The Island is from a dozen to fifteen miles across, with a deeply indented shore and a bold mountain ridge traversing its longest axis, intersected by a dozen deep, ice-excavated gorges. A bridge connects it with the mainland, and makes it one of the principal termini of Maine's extensive State-road system. Though but recently opened to automobiles, owing to the summer residents' delight in horses, motoring has now become the principal swift means of locomotion, bringing the whole Island into close touch with Bar Harbor for every purpose of social life or out-door excursion.

Bar Harbor offers features, scenic and social both, of unique attractiveness as a resting-place on any eastern tour to coast or mountains. From it as a starting-point interesting trips may be made by motor to what but lately seemed far-distant points upon the mainland—to Castine, beautifully situated upon Penobscot Bay, and rich in historic association; to lakes in the interior famous for their fishing and wild woodland beauty, or to the Canadian border down the eastern coast. Motoring from the White Mountains it is but two days' journey; from Portland or Poland Springs a single day will bring one to Bar Harbor, though the journey may be pleasantly broken by stopping at the famous Samoset Hotel at Rockland, or other points of interest upon the way. From Bar Harbor again to the Kineo House, on Moosehead Lake, and back is a delightful two or three days' trip; while even Quebec may be reached from it easily and pleasantly in two days' motoring by those who wish to make a more extended tour. A State road just completed leads from Bangor, at tidal water on the Penobscot River—a distance of but fifty miles—to Bar Harbor; and of its own roads, which compare favorably with any in New England, the town is justly proud.

Yachting, Boating, and Fishing

Bar Harbor is an important yachting center to which the great New York and Eastern Yachting Squadrons make an annual cruise, while boats of every yachting type, from ocean-going steamers to little sailing craft that the owners man themselves fill the harbor full all summer long. Naval Squadrons, too, of the Country make frequent stay here, for Frenchman's Bay is an important point in the eyes of naval strategists, as well as a favorite harborage for officers and crews, and it is a glorious sight upon a summer's day to see one of these giant battle-fleets slowly steaming up the Bay in formidable majesty, or to behold a white-winged yachting squadron pursue its inward or its outward way, lazily or swiftly, as the wind may serve, in daintily grace. For those who love the water, there is sailing and motor boating of extraordinary variety and interest round about the Island and through the sheltered waterways that lead from it unbrokenly by a maze of islands to Penobscot Bay, while the deep-sea fishing of the region is famous from its first exploration in the fifteen hundreds on [*sic*].

Swimming and Bathing

The Bar Harbor Swimming Pool has a wide reputation for its gay cosmopolitanism and social attractions. Besides its large, open air, salt-water pool, it has a well-appointed club-house, with restaurant and ball-room. There are frequent dances, and music that recalls some well-run foreign watering-place or spa. The swimming-pool itself is the scene from time to time of aquatic tournaments which are well-worth witnessing. Visitors at the hotels may readily secure admission, as also to the Kebo Valley Golf Club, through the manager of their hotel, or introduction by a member.

Good bathing in the open, sun-warmed waters of the Upper Bay may also be obtained by motoring to Woodland Park, close beyond Salisbury Cove, and a swift, pleasant drive along good roads. There is a restaurant adjoining for those who wish to stay for lunch or motor out. The scenery along this shore, wholly different from that of the Island's seaward face, is of peculiar charm and interest, and should be visited both here and at the famous "Ovens," not far distant.

Golfing and Tennis

No holiday resort would be complete nowadays without its golf links, and in this respect Bar Harbor takes high place. The course is situated in Kebo Valley, at the mountain's foot, a short drive or pleasant walk-out from the town, and has won the high encomium of noted players. A nine-hole golf course as yet, a movement is well underway for its extension to eighteen holes. The greens are among the best in the country, while the course generally lies over land of an unusually interesting golfing character. Those who have once played on these links return to them year after year with constant pleasure, and when extended to a full course of eighteen holes no other will outrank it in reputation among first-class players. Adjoining the Club House, too, are excellent tennis courts, where, during the season as also at the Swimming Pool, tournaments are played that bring famous champions to compete and brilliant crowds to witness.

Music and Art

Art is fittingly enshrined amid exquisite natural surroundings at the Building of Arts, placed on an elevation looking southward through the mountain gap which opens a direct and striking way from Bar Harbor to the ocean front. Carefully planned by a committee of summer residents, who sought especially an ideal home for music and a background for the performance of world-famous artists who frequent the Island, it is a perfect example of Greek architecture that might appropriately crown the Acropolis or look down upon the groves of Mount Parnassus. Here during a single season may be heard such masters of their art as Paderewski, Kreisler, Schelling and Hoffmann. Distinguished dramatic entertainments, staged often in the noble grove of pines outside, have been given here as well, and flower shows rich in the brilliant color of the Island's summer bloom. Though but five minutes' walk from one of Bar Harbor's gayest and most crowded centers of fashionable hotel life, no house is visible from the Building site, but only woods and mountains, and the broad golf lawns; and while as one lingers after beautiful and noble music, the scene is one which leaves a deep impression.

Library

What is probably the most perfect Village Library in the country, with a delightful reading-room, and open, well-filled shelves, was given to Bar Harbor some years since by Mrs.

Morris K. Jesup, of New York, in memory of her husband and their long association with the Island's summer life. It is a joy to all who seek a quiet and studious spot in which to read or work. A beautiful old-fashioned, perennial garden surrounds the building on three sides, and is worth a visit at any time during summer. Within, upon the right, an interesting loaned exhibition of etchings, prints and similar art objects has been carried on of late, changing from week to week the season through. Opposite the entrance door, in the rotunda, is a striking bronze bust of a beloved summer resident and ardent lover of the Island's wilder ways—the late Dr. S. Weir Mitchell, of Philadelphia.

National Scenic Park

Bar Harbor has a splendid natural park in the noble reservation that now takes in the greater part of the Island's mountain system, and which it is hoped by its founders may presently be taken over as a free gift by the United States Government, to form a national monument, the first on the Atlantic Coast. Superb in bold and varied landscape, it extends from the very borders of Bar Harbor village, far across the Island to the summer colonies upon its southern shore, and includes, besides the mountain range, the watershed of Eagle Lake and Jordan Pond, which, lying at an elevation of nearly 300 feet above the sea, furnish water respectively to Bar Harbor and Seal Harbor. The preservation for all time in wild and unspoiled beauty of the mountainous center of the Island, with its rugged hills and valleys, its lakes and forests, and many exquisite features of natural beauty, is a high achievement the importance of which must grow swiftly manifest. It affords a guarantee, moreover, that the wonderful flora and native fauna of this most fertile spot will not only be preserved in perpetuity, but will, under proper care and guardianship increase and multiply.

Gardens

Bar Harbor is unquestionably a wonderful garden spot. The fine old-fashioned plants of English gardens and the new introductions from China and Japan both flourish here as nowhere else in North America. Why it is so is a mystery, but the fact is certain, and one has only to see the plants in bloom and in their vigorous seasonal growth to recognize it. The flowers are more brilliant and come in more generous abundance than they do in other places, and the gardens are correspondingly more beautiful. There are a number of already famous private gardens at Bar Harbor, and the owners are generally glad to have them seen, at proper times and seasons. They are worth seeking access to at almost any time in summer, for there is no barren moment in a Bar Harbor garden, no interlude when blossom has ceased.

Older than most of the private gardens on the Island, and well-worth a visit for their extended scale and striking landscape setting are the Hardy Plant Gardens of the Mount Desert Nurseries, opposite the junction of the Otter Creek and Schooner Head roads on Main Street. These always one may freely see and wander through at will. And from the brilliant Rock Garden and other blooms of early summer to the magnificent display of Phlox these gardens show towards the season's end, or of deep blue Monkshood and Autumnal Asters even later, there is no moment when a visit to them, as to any of the greater private gardens, will not well repay the lover of abundant bloom and hardy plants.

Paths

A unique feature at Bar Harbor lies in the Island's wonderful mountain paths that "look upon the sea." There is nothing like them elsewhere in the east, not heights that show like these the "ocean's vast expanse"—a sight of singular grandeur as one beholds it from them, with a singularly fitting foreground, too, of ancient lichen-covered rock and vegetation rich in the forms and somber beauty of the north. Now taking a level way through wooded valleys, now climbing cliffs that but for them were perilous, these paths have endless variety, and are besides extraordinary in the primeval wildness of the nature into which they quickly plunge one.

Hotels

Pre-eminent in luxury among hotels of the larger scale is the Malvern, created thirty years ago by the genius of de Grasse Fox of Philadelphia—inheritor of two famous names—which has been the center ever since of Bar Harbor's gayest and most fashionable hotel life. Rebuilt and enlarged, with an admirable cuisine and every comfort, and with picturesque dependent cottages clustered round it, it is in every sense a modern house today, whose only drawback springs from its popularity and the difficulty one may find in getting rooms at the season's height.

Modern and luxurious too, and excellently run, but on a smaller scale is the de Gregoire, named for the first owners of this portion of the Island, a Frenchman and his wife of ancient lineage now buried at Hull's Cove, who claimed it under an old grant from Louis XIV, which was confirmed to them by the Commonwealth of Massachusetts when Maine was but a province.

Another center of hotel life, with pleasant cottages to rent around it, is the Louisburg, whose name stands high for comfort, and which lies but a couple of minutes' walk away from the shore path, whose value as a park resource to the hotel guest or dweller in a rented cottage in the town it would be difficult to over-estimate.

The Newport House—recently acquired by the Maine Central Railroad as part of a splendid building site, looking across the bay and harbor, for a new hotel whose plans, designed on a magnificent scale have been already drawn; the St. Sauverur and Belmont, upon Mt. Desert St., complete the list of present large hotels, but there are abundant opportunities besides for renting rooms and houses in the town. Particulars in regard to these the Bureau of Information, on Maine St., most gladly furnish, or answer any questions as to hotels, their rooms and prices.

Houses and Cottages to Rent

The extraordinary faculty Bar Harbor has of attaching people to it and making them wish to make themselves a home there, even for brief periods or occasionally, if no more be possible, has led correspondingly in the course of years to numerous homes to rent, of every type and price. These vary from stately mansions, built as the abode of wealth in splendid situations upon shore or hill, to attractive bungalows outside the town or cottages within it. In this respect the opportunity Bar Harbor affords is probably unique, owing to its own remarkable variety of landscape, and to the scarcely less striking differences in character, in taste and fortune that have existed from the start among its summer visitors.

Institutions and Business Features

Bar Harbor is well-supplied with churches, the Episcopal Congregational and Catholic being conspicuously placed on Mt. Desert Street; the Unitarian and Baptist on Ledgelawn Avenue, not far away; the Methodist on School Street. It has fine Young Men's and Young Women's Christian Association buildings, upon Mt. Desert Street also, which do most useful work. It has a pleasant and well shaded village green and a delightful children's park, whose recent transformation from an unsightly wilderness has been the gift and labor of love of Mrs. John S. Harrison, of Philadelphia; and it has another gift of priceless future value to the town in what is said to be the best athletic field in Maine.

The new Post Office on Cottage Street is an excellent piece of Government architecture, handsome and commodious, and built appropriately of the native granite, one of the finest, as it is the most enduring of building materials; while the High School building on the same street beyond, is one in which the town takes special pride, and is well worth a visit, not only for its architectural distinction and fitness to a High School's needs, but for the valuable educational work that year by year is being carried on in it.

An admirably equipped Hospital, well-placed and near the shore, is open all the year. Supported mainly by the liberality of summer residents, it has an honorary staff of doctors and surgeons of national repute drawn from the summer colony, besides the regular practitioners of the place, of whom there are several of established reputation in Bar Harbor.

The Fire Department, splendidly equipped and housed, is remarkably efficient, as occasional experience has proved. It can be relied [missing text]

Bar Harbor is well-supplied with excellent markets and general stores, as well as, in summer time, branches of leading New York, Washington and Boston firms, able to fill the most exacting needs. There are also two excellently managed banks on Main Street, the Bar Harbor Banking and Trust Company and the First National Bank of Bar Harbor.

Two local newspapers, the Bar Harbor Times and Record, help to keep visitors and residents in touch with all of seasonal or local interest, while during the summer season, with its swift and frequent trains, the New York and Boston daily papers seem to reach Bar Harbor almost as soon as printed.

The Bar Harbor Bureau of Information, established by the town in connection with the local Board of Trade, will answer any question asked by mail as well as furnish any information required by visitors or others. It also seeks to keep a full registry of arrivals at and departures from Bar Harbor.

Magnificent photographs of Bar Harbor views in wide variety, taken by Mr. George B. King, of Boston, may be freely seen, or obtained, if one desire, at the Mount Desert Studio on Main Street, opposite the Athletic Field. Regarded simply as an exhibition of the Island scenery in its most beautiful and striking aspects, these photographs should not be left unseen.

Social Clubs

There are several social clubs at Bar Harbor, the oldest of which is the finely situated Reading Room, close to the Maine Central wharf, with the earliest summer residence upon the Island on its seaward side; while the gayest is the Swimming pool, three minutes' walk away towards the west. The Kebo Valley Golf Club lies outside the town, in a wonderful situation at the Mountain's base, but readily accessible by foot or motor.

Selected Bibliography

Aldrich, Nelson W., Jr. *Old Money, The Mythology of America's Upper Class*. New York: Alfred A. Knopf, 1988.

Aslet, Clive, *The American Country House*. New Haven: Yale University Press, 1990.

Baldwin, Letitia. "Savage Beauties, the Summer Palaces of Frederick L. Savage." *Downeast* (February 1996): 32–37.

Belanger, Pamela J. *Inventing Acadia, Artists and Tourists at Mount Desert*. Rockland: The Farnsworth Art Museum, 1999.

Bryant, William Cullen, ed. *Picturesque America: or, The Land We Live In*. New York: D. Appleton and Company, 1872.

Carter, Robert. *Summer Cruise of the Coast of New England*. Boston: Crosby and Nichols, 1864.

Cromwell, Jarvis. *Our Family, an Octogenarian's Letter to His Grandchildren*. Dalton, Mass.: Studley Press, 1978.

Cromwell, Mrs. Lincoln. *A Glimpse of Northeast Harbor in the Nineties*. Typescript, Northeast Harbor Library, 1950.

DeCosta, B. F. *Rambles in Mount Desert with Sketches of Travel on the New-England Coast, from Isles of Shoals to Grand Menan*. New York: A. D. F. Randolph, 1871.

Dorr, George B. *Acadia National Park, Its Origin and Background*. Bangor: Burr Printing Company, 1942.

Eliot, Charles W. *Charles Eliot, Landscape Architect*. Amherst: University of Massachusetts Press, 1999.

———. *The Right Development of Mount Desert*. Privately printed, 1904.

Gerdts, William H. "American Landscape Painting: Critical Judgments, 1730–1845." *The American Art Journal* 17 (winter 1985): 28–59.

Gilborn, Craig. *Adirondack Camps, Homes Away from Home, 1850–1950*. Syracuse: Syracuse University Press, 2000.

Hale, Richard Walden, Jr. *The Story of Bar Harbor*. New York: Ives Washburn, 1949.

Hansen, Gunnar, ed. *Mount Desert, an Informal History*. Mount Desert: The Town of Mount Desert, 1989.

Hansen, Gunnar. *Not a Common House, a History of St. Mary's-by-the-Sea*. Privately printed, 1981.

Hay, John and Peter Farb. *The Atlantic Shore*. New York: Harper & Row, 1966.

Helfrich, G. W. and Gladys O'Neil. *Lost Bar Harbor*. Camden: Down East Books, 1982.

Hill, Ruth Ann. *Discovering Old Bar Harbor and Acadia National Park, an Unconventional History and Guide*. Camden, Maine: Down East Books, 1996.

Hindle, Brooke, ed. *America's Wooden Age: Aspects of Its Early Technology*. Tarrytown: Sleepy Hollow Restorations, 1985.

Holden, Wheaton A. "The Peabody Touch: Peabody and Stearns of Boston, 1870–1917." *Journal of the Society of Architectural Historians* 32 (May 1973): 114–132.

James, Henry. *Charles W. Eliot, President of Harvard University, 1869–1909*. Boston: Houghton Mifflin, 1930.

Kelly, Franklin. *Frederic Edwin Church and the North American Landscape, 1845–1860*. Ph.D. diss., University of Delaware, 1985.

Knowles, Jared A. *An Exploration of the Colonial Revival Through Selected Works of Fred Savage, Architect*. M.F.A. Thesis, Savannah College of Art and Design, 1994.

Koelsch, William A. "Antebellum Harvard Students and the Recreational Exploration of the New England Landscape." *Journal of Historical Geography* 8 (October 1982): 362–372.

Kohlstedt, Sally Gregory, ed. *The Origins of Natural Science in America, the Essays of George Brown Goode*. Washington, D.C.: Smithsonian Institution Press, 1991.

Lawrence, Henry W. "Southern Spas: Source of the American Resort Tradition." *Landscape* 27 (1983): 1–12.

McLane, Charles B. *Islands of the Mid-Maine Coast,* vol 2, *Mount Desert to Machias Bay*. Falmouth, Maine: The Kennebec River Press, 1989.

Mazlish, Anne, ed. *The Tracy Log Book, 1855, A Month in Summer*. Bar Harbor: Acadia Publishing, 1997.

Morison, Samuel Eliot. *Spring Tides*. Cambridge: The Riverside Press, 1965.

———. *The Story of Mount Desert Island, Maine*. Boston: Little, Brown, 1960.

Ochsner, Jeffrey Karl and Thomas C. Hubka. "H. H. Richardson: The Design of the William Watts Sherman House." *Journal of the Society of Architectural Historians* 51 (June 1992): 121–145.

Nash, Roderick. *Wilderness and the American Mind*. New Haven and London: Yale University Press, 1973.

Roth, Leland M. *Shingle Styles, Innovation and Tradition in American Architecture, 1874–1982*. New York: Harry N. Abrams, 1999.

Reed, Roger G. *A Delight to All Who Know It, The Maine Summer Architecture of William R. Emerson*. Portland: Maine Citizens for Historic Preservation, 1995.

———. "Bar Harbor Cottages, 1868–1940, a List of Summer Cottages with Architects and Builders." (Fall 1988, revised February 1992). Maine Historic Preservation Commission. Augusta, Maine.

Reynolds, Emily Phillips. "My Recollections of Grandfather and Grandmother and Their Family." (1982). Northeast Harbor Library, Maine.

Rhoads, William B. "The Discovery of America's Architectural Past, 1874–1914." *Studies in the History of Art* 35 (1990): 23–39.

Rogers, Robert William. "Rudolf E. Brunnow, Gentleman and Scholar." *The Methodist Review* (January–February 1918): 66–75.

Roths, Jaylene B. "Fred Savage, the Cottage Builder." *The History Journal of the Mount Desert Historical Society* II (1999): 38–56.

Savage, Augustus Chase. *Memories of a Lifetime* (1902). Northeast Harbor Library.

Savage, Fred Lincoln. *Attractive Summer Homes and Scenes*. Privately printed, [1903?].

Savage, Rick. "To All Who May Inquire." (n.d.) Northeast Harbor Library.

Saylor, Henry H. *Journal of the American Institute of Architects, The AIA's First Hundred Years*. Washington: AIA, 1957.

Scully, Vincent J., Jr. *The Shingle Style and the Stick Style: Architectural Theory and Design from Downing to the Origins of Wright*. New Haven: Yale University Press, 1955.

———. *The Shingle Style Today, or the Historian's Revenge*. New York: George Braziller, 1974.

Shettleworth, Earle G., Jr. *The Summer Cottages of Islesboro, 1890–1930*. Islesboro, Maine: Islesboro Historical Society, 1989.

Shettleworth, Earle G., Jr., ed. and Roger Reed, associate ed. *A Biographical Dictionary of Architects in Maine*. Augusta: Maine Historic Preservation Commission, 1984, et seq.

Sweetser, M. F. *Chisholm's Mount-Desert Guide-Book*. Portland: Chisholm Brothers, 1888.

Thoreau, Henry David. *The Maine Woods*. New York: Bramhall House, 1950.

Varney, George J. *A Gazetteer of the State of Maine*. Boston: B. B. Russell, 1881.

[Vaughan, W.W.]. *Northeast Harbor Reminiscences*. N.p.: White and Home, 1930.

Wilmerding, John. *The Artist's Mount Desert, American Painters on the Maine Coast*. Princeton: Princeton University Press, 1994.

Withey, Henry F. and Elsie Rathburn Withey. *Biographical Dictionary of American Architects (Deceased)*. Los Angeles: Hennessey & Ingalls, 1970.

Index

following pages: Upper Hadlock Pond
(page 302), Monument Cove (page 303),
twilight from Cadillac Mountain (page
304), all Acadia National Park